50

Children's Sermons

50
Children's Sermons

Graham R. Hodges

ABINGDON PRESS

New York • *Nashville*

50 CHILDREN'S SERMONS

Copyright © MCMLVII by Abingdon Press

Library of Congress Catalog Card Number: 57-12390

The sermon "The Man Who Could See Only Money"
was originally published in *The Lutheran*, January 13,
1954, and is used by permission.

C

SET UP, PRINTED, AND BOUND BY THE
PARTHENON PRESS, AT NASHVILLE,
TENNESSEE, UNITED STATES OF AMERICA

PREFACE

IN THESE PAGES ARE CHILDREN'S SERMONS I USED WHILE PASTOR of two small churches—the First Congregational churches of Ticonderoga and Crown Point, New York.

Throughout these talks I have tried not to use the "talking down" attitude so common and yet so hard to avoid. Also, I have tried, without one hundred per cent success, to avoid preaching to the adults by way of the children. This process isn't necessary. For if a good idea or great truth is expressed as it should be—simply—it will hit child and grownup alike. We have no record of "children's sermons" in the four Gospels.

For whatever they are worth in leading "the little ones" to God, their Father, I offer these messages.

This volume is dedicated to Mr. and Mrs. F. B. Hodges of Wesson, Mississippi, who taught me most of what I know about God.

GRAHAM R. HODGES

CONTENTS

7

1. The Earth's Oldest Chemical

IN MY HAND I HOLD A GLASS OF THE EARTH'S OLDEST CHEMICAL. It's one you used this very morning—that is, if you washed your hands and faces before coming to church.

Correct! This is a glass of water. Just ordinary, plain water, as it came from the faucet.

Water is the earth's oldest chemical, and perhaps the most valuable and necessary for man's existence. Scientists tell us that the water we use today—yes, the water in this very glass—is exactly the same chemical it was billions of years ago. When the dinosaurs roamed the earth, they drank and wallowed in this very water. The saber-toothed tiger lapped it up.

Of course it's changed form and traveled a bit in its day. It has been ice, sleet, hail, snow, dew, rain, fog, ocean water, river water, lake water, creek water, well water, and lots of other kinds. It was in Africa, Asia, the South Pacific, the Arctic, the Antarctic, and all over the seven seas. You could write geography, history, and science books, filling a whole room just on the places this small bit of water has been, the people it has touched, the things it's done.

Water hasn't changed a bit in its chemical composition. Other chemical compounds do change—but not water. God must have planned it that way, for we must have plentiful water.

You can make water dirty, muddy, or impure. You can dissolve other chemicals such as salt or sugar in it. But the water itself always returns to its original state—two parts hydrogen and one part oxygen. God, in his wonderful way, purifys water over and over again.

His powerful sun shines on earth and sea, drawing water upward in purest vapor form, and then releases it for our use in snow, rain, and hail. Each year, the scientists tell us, 1/3,000 of the water in the oceans rises into the sky as vapor and falls again as pure, clear liquid.

And, like the water, God can purify us too. When we have bad, ugly thoughts, he can forgive us, if we ask him. When we are nasty tempered, we can become sweet again with his help.

If we're truly sorry for our sins, God can take them away forever. He can cleanse all the bad, dirty, ugly feelings, acts, and thoughts. For you see, like the indestructible water I hold in my hand, the human soul lasts a long time. And God can cleanse and purify our souls again and again, if we ask him.

Each night when we lie down to sleep, we should first get down on our knees beside the bed and tell God what we've done wrong, ask his pardon, and request help to be better next day. Then we can rise the next morning with clean hearts.

Just as he purifies the water, God will cleanse our everlasting souls.

2. Walking in the Other Man's Shoes

OUR NORTH AMERICAN INDIANS HAD GREAT SPIRITUAL INSIGHT. WE forget this when we think of them only as blood-thirsty savages, always ready to go on war parties. I'm glad to see the movies and television programs picturing the Indians more like the white men—just people, some good, some bad, and some in between.

One great Indian saying was this: "Let me not judge my brother until I have walked for two moons in his shoes." Maybe they said moccasins instead of shoes, but it means the same.

Walking in the other fellow's shoes means trying to put yourself in his place. Often we condemn or talk about others in a harsh way. Later, we find out we're all wrong. Then it's too late to recall the words and the damage they have done.

We can never really know what other people are like inside. I once knew a boy we all regarded as a horrible "pill," if you know what I mean. What a character! Later my own parents explained that he was badly treated at home. After that I had more sympathy for him. In my own mind, I walked in his shoes, as the Indians suggested.

Perhaps you know some boy or girl who's afraid. Afraid to play, afraid to speak up in class, afraid of other children. Try to imagine what it's like to be afraid of everything. Then give that boy or girl lots of encouragement and friendship.

In your mind, walk in their shoes. You'll never be sorry if you do.

3. Overcoming Your Weak Points

ONLY TWO MEN IN THE HISTORY OF THE AMERICAN LEAGUE HAVE been unanimously voted "the most valuable player of the year." Every sports writer in the United States voted for Al Rosen in 1953 and Mickey Mantle in 1956. Both these men helped put their teams in the World Series.

Al Rosen is the man we'll think about today. One of the top hitters, he's one of the all-time great players of the game. It wouldn't be surprising if he'd wind up in the Baseball Hall of Fame in Cooperstown, New York.

Somebody asked Al Rosen once how he became the great player he is. Naturally, he had lots of natural ability. We know that. But here is his answer to this question: "I work on my weak points and correct them."

Not a bad method, for it made him among the top big leaguers, the first man to be voted the most valuable man in the American League, without a single vote against him.

And on the ball field he worked on his weak points. He studied, practiced, and practiced still more, brushing up and perfecting every detail of catching, throwing, running bases, and batting.

First of all, he had to recognize his weaknesses. Most of us don't care to have our weak points known. Not Al Rosen. He welcomed advice on how he could become better.

If somebody who really cares for us—our mother, father, teacher, scoutmaster, minister, or a friend—tells us how we could improve, how do we react? Some of us say, "They're nuts! There's nothing wrong with me!"

If we're wise, we'll think about what they say. Perhaps they're right. They can see us better than we see ourselves.

Suppose you want to play outfield on your ball team. You can field pretty well, but you can't hit. What's the best thing to do as an ambitious outfielder? Learn to hit, of course!

Or suppose you want to bring your grades up, but arithmetic is your worst enemy? Hit that arithmetic hard! That's the way, and the only way.

You know, Jesus had the most trouble with people who thought they were perfect. These people were called Pharisees. They just knew they were right. Nothing wrong with them— or so they thought.

Once I had a wonderful schoolteacher. She thought so much of me that she stopped me in the hall one day, looked me straight in the eye, and said: "Graham, you're a fine boy, but you've got one big fault. You put things off." I knew she was right, and replied: "Yes, ma'am, I'll try to do better." Ever since then I've always been grateful to this teacher, who cared so much for me that she made a suggestion for my improvement.

No matter what you do, find your weak points. Practice on them. Make them your strong points. That's what Al Rosen did.

4. Stepping Ahead of the Crowd

RECENTLY I WAS READING THE LIFE STORY OF THE WORLD'S GREATEST contralto singer. Who is this person?

The world's greatest contralto is a woman and a Negro. She is Marian Anderson. She grew up with two strikes against her, you might say. In a nation where white people run things, she was colored, And, as a poor girl, she had little money for music lessons.

How she struggled, sacrificed, worked, got the training she needed, is in itself a long story. Once an organization wouldn't let her sing in an auditorium in Washington, D.C., because she was colored. Sounds crazy, but it's the truth. When people heard about this outrage, an out-of-door concert was arranged in Washington, and more came to hear her there than could have crowded inside.

But it's not as a great singer that I want to present Marian Anderson to you today, but as a great person. For she *is* a very great person as well.

In her life story she gives this bit of advice: "When we are afraid to do the right thing, and yet we know it's the right thing, then go ahead and do it. Others who were afraid, too, will then join you, and then others. All they want is somebody who's bold enough to take the first step, then they'll follow."

I know that lots of times you're afraid to do the right thing, to stand up for the right. How do I know? Because I was a boy once and know how you feel.

All around you, in school and at play, are others who are sometimes afraid to do what they know is right. It takes courage of the best kind to step out ahead of the crowd. Other kids laugh at you. Some might call you "sissy." Even your friends might think you're making a fool of yourself.

But the world is as good as it is today because great leaders did dare to do the right—to change the old ways for new ways.

Marian Anderson became great by daring to do right. In your own way you can become great too. No matter how afraid you are, follow your conscience. Before long others will say, "That's the way I feel too."

5. God's Windows

RECENTLY I STOPPED IN OUR CHURCH JUST AT DUSK. EVENING SHADOWS were falling fast. I sat down in the back pew for a moment of silence. As I did, I noticed a strange thing that occurs every night here in the church after sunset.

The stained-glass windows seemed to gather every ray of light, concentrate it, and pass it inside, enriched and beautified by the various colors. As darkness deepened, the windows grew darker, too, but still glowed even more beautifully, far lovelier than at midday when the sun shines brightest.

I thought: How like human beings these windows are. All about us is some kind of darkness. There is the darkness of fear, the darkness of ignorance, of sin, of hatred, and other kinds of darkness.

But Christian people are supposed to catch the light of God, however dim it might seem; and by letting it shine through their lives, pass it on, enriched, to other people. Like the various colors of stained-glass windows, you and I and millions of other people are all different. No two alike.

Yet, we all receive the same kind of light—the identical love of God. If our lives are unattractive, covered with evil thoughts and deeds, then very little light shines through to those hungry for it.

But if we have the kind of Christian character Christ had,

14

then God's light shines through lovelier than ever. We are God's windows. Others see God through us.

We can reveal God to others or hide him from them. The kind of light they get depends in part on what kind we let pass through.

Christ was God's perfect window, you might say. In fact, in the Bible he is called "the light of the world." Had he allowed his life to be sinful, the world would have very little light indeed. We wouldn't celebrate Christmas or Easter. We would have no churches. Our world would be a different and worse place to live in.

Christ wants us to take his light and pass it on. We see God through him. Others see God through us.

God needs human windows who'll let his light shine through as darkness comes on. He needs us for this.

6. *Keep On Trying*

DOES GOD EVER GET DISCOURAGED? WHAT DO YOU THINK?

Even if this seems a strange question, it's at least worth thinking about.

For, if I were God, I think I'd be very discouraged. Apparently he is very patient, though. God has been making human beings for thousands of years. Many thousands, for scientists are discovering the remains of civilizations and primitive human beings more than a hundred thousand years old.

And everyone of these human beings, for all these thousands of years, has disobeyed God in some way, just like we do today.

Adam and Eve did. David did. Solomon, the wisest man who ever lived, broke God's laws too. Only Jesus Christ was perfect.

So, you'd think God would give up and quit. But he doesn't.

Of all the people living on this planet we call Earth, not one is perfect. No, not a single one obeys God in every way.

Still, our heavenly Father goes on creating new human beings. This takes patience of the highest kind.

Great people are patient too. They work hard at their jobs, striving to do their best. That's why most of them are great. Don Hutson, for example, was the greatest pass receiver the football game has ever seen. He played with the University of Alabama and then for years with the Green Bay Packers. He could snatch a pass from any angle—right side, left side, overhead, or any style you please.

Sure, Don Hutson was a natural-born athlete. He was good to start with. But that's not why he was the greatest pass catcher ever seen. Listen to his story, his secret: "For every pass I caught in a game I had practiced catching a thousand!"

Imagine that! A thousand practice catches for every good one completed in a game.

Thomas Alva Edison, America's greatest inventor, was a very patient man too. He invented the phonograph, the electric power system we use today, the motion picture, and the electric-light bulb. Edison failed five thousand times in trying to find just the right filament to use in the light bulb. Five thousand failures. Then success. Five thousand discouragements. Then, the light bulb.

Most of us get discouraged and quit a task after five or six trials. That's why many of us fail in even small tasks.

In your arithmetic, your sports, your music lessons, your Girl Scout and Boy Scout troops, your reading assignments, your chores at home—you usually do well only if you keep trying.

Remember God's great patience with us. Remember Don Hutson's thousand practice catches to every one on the field. Remember Thomas Edison's five thousand failures before he invented the electric light bulb. And keep trying at whatever you're wanting to do well.

16

7. *Autumn Leaves and Elderly People*

WILL YOU EVER GROW OLD? YES, YOU WILL, IF YOUR WISH COMES true. For nobody wishes to die young. That means we want to grow old, doesn't it?

I know that growing old, stiff, gray-haired, and feeble is the least of your ambitions. But more and more people are growing old, and more and more people are actually having a good time as older people, believe it or not.

I'd like to pass on to you the secret of being loved, respected, and happy after sixty-five. No, you haven't much interest now in the subject. I don't blame you, for I don't have too much either. I tell myself it's a long way off.

So, don't worry about growing old. That happens automatically, without any effort on your part. But just take this bit of information I'm about to give you, tuck it in the back of your mind, and keep it safe.

The secret is this: The kind of person you are now is very likely the kind of person you will be when you're old! Sounds complicated, I know. But it's true, just the same.

If you're kind, generous, of service to others, charitable, brave, and honest now and during the next few years, then you'll be a very lovable person when you're sixty-five.

In a way, people are like autumn leaves. Each fall, green leaves turn into their various lovely colors. Scientists are puzzled as to why one turns brown, another red, another yellow, and so on. But they think they turn these colors because of the different chemical content in each leaf.

For example, the maple is about our most beautiful fall tree. Its brightest colors are red and yellow. The maple leaf has a high sugar content—filled with sweetness, you might say.

If your life is filled with sweetness—with the kind of thoughts, acts, and motives you'd be proud of, then your autumn years, the last ones in your life, will be beautiful.

On the other hand, I notice that individuals who're unkind, stingy, and mean during their youth and adult lives are cranky old people—the kind you have to leave alone. These people have thought, all their lives, just about themselves.

I know a man who bawls his wife out if supper isn't ready exactly at six o'clock. How'd you like to live with him when he's seventy years old and meaner than ever? What a grumpy old character *he's* going to be!

I also know a woman who likes to bake cookies and goodies for children. I can predict that she'll make a lovely old lady.

Right now, today, tomorrow, this week, this year you're determining what kind of old person you'll be. Just as the tree stores up in its leaves the chemicals that give it an ugly or lovely color in the fall, so you're storing up the kind of life that will be ugly or beautiful years and years from now.

Do you want to be loved, respected, and liked when you are old? Now's the time to start!

8. *Good Christians Do Get Angry*

IS IT A SIN TO GET ANGRY? IS IT WRONG TO LOSE YOUR TEMPER? Absolutely not. Provided, you get angry or lose your temper over the right thing.

Suppose you have a brother or sister. Perhaps you really do and don't have to suppose it. Suppose at dinner tonight your mother gives you a small piece of cake or pie and your brother or sister the larger piece. Losing your temper over that is wrong. And most of us lose our temper over just such petty annoyances as that.

Many auto accidents are caused by anger. Often very petty anger. One driver is rude to another. Then the second driver, to get even, takes his anger out on a third. And so on. Within a matter of minutes some innocent person is badly hurt or killed. Far fetched? Not a bit. Such accidents, temper caused, happen every day on American highways. Practically every large hospital has injured persons recovering from just such so-called "accidents."

To illustrate why a Christian can get angry, let's take an imaginary trip to New Orleans, Louisiana. The time—more than 125 years ago. There in the heart of the French Quarter is a large stone—the slave auction block. On this block, the symbol of a slave system we will never see again, were placed men, women, boys, and girls. They were auctioned off to the highest bidder. They were closely examined to see how much work they could do. An able-bodied young man brought a thousand dollars.

Year after year this went on. Some people said it was wrong, but saw nothing they could do about it. People who called themselves Christian walked by the slave auction on their way to the lovely church just a few feet away. Some probably bought a slave after leaving a church service.

Then, one day, a tall, gangling young man came to town. He came from Illinois. His name was Abraham Lincoln. It is reported that when *he* saw the slave auction, so inhuman and cruel, he said, "I'll smash it!" Years later Abraham Lincoln wrote the Emancipation Proclamation, setting the American Negro free from legal bondage.

One notable feature of Lincoln's character was the good-natured way he took jokes, criticisms, and even lies about himself. Things that make most of us literally boil inside, he took with a joke.

But the injustices and cruelties he saw inflicted on other people, especially helpless folk like the slaves, made him burn with

19

anger. And instead of just getting angry and blowing off steam, so to speak, he did something about the injustices.

What makes you angry? Just petty annoyances? Or do you get upset when you see wrongs committed against innocent, helpless people?

The world badly needs angry Christians, not peevish Christians. Yes, I'd say it's not a sin to get angry. Sometimes it's a sin *not* to get angry.

When you lose your temper, lose it over principle, not the little selfish incidents. Little people get angry over little things. Big people get angry over big things. Are you big or little?

9. Giving Others the Credit

IN 1954 THE NEW YORK GIANTS TOOK THE WORLD SERIES FROM THE Cleveland Indians in four straight games. The Indians had a great team that year, and it took some playing to beat them in four straight.

In the second game of the series, two men were hailed as the stars—"Dusty" Rhodes, the great hitter, and Johnny Antonelli, who pitched the *Giants* to victory. Naturally, the crowd went wild over both.

At the game's end, the *Giants'* dressing room was crowded— all the people you see on television pushed in. Fans, autograph seekers, and especially newspaper reporters and photographers. And mostly to see "Dusty" Rhodes and Johnny Antonelli.

But over in the corner was another hero—the man who might well have deserved to be called the real hero. Not a single photographer took his picture. And only one reporter asked him any questions. His name was Wes Westrum.

No, you'll probably never hear the name of Wes Westrum. But he, Westrum, was the hero of the series.

Westrum played catcher. And it's the catcher who runs the ball team on the field. He's like the quarterback in a football game.

Ever watch the pitcher out on the mound, just before the wind-up? He stands there silently, gazing toward the batter. Actually, he's getting the signal for this or that kind of pitch. The catcher signals a curve, a fast ball, a slider, or whatever he thinks the batter can't hit. Then the pitcher does his best to deliver the order.

From behind the plate, Wes Westrum masterminded the 1954 World Series victory for the *Giants*. Johnny Antonelli threw whatever Westrum called for.

Who should get the most credit? That's for you to decide. But do you think Westrum, the catcher, should get any less credit than Antonelli, the pitcher? Hardly. But, in the public mind, it was Antonelli who won the ball game.

Was Wes Westrum peeved or jealous? Not on your life. Listen to what he told the single reporter who thought enough of him to ask his opinion after the final game: "We won the game. What more could anybody want?"

As you grow older, you'll find yourself in Wes Westrum's place more than once. No, perhaps not playing in the World Series.

But in this respect: You'll work hard and make some project successful. Then somebody else will get the credit.

Unfair? It happens every day.

Perhaps you'll do the hard, dirty work in some organization and nobody says to you: "What a fine job! You deserve a lot of credit!"

Well, take this advice: Don't get sore about it. Instead, take a joyful attitude that you could do your part.

And in the long run you'll be recognized for your worth, provided you don't quit too soon.

10. You Can't Get Something for Nothing

MANY YEARS AGO, WHEN I KNEW VERY LITTLE ABOUT THE COST of things, I went to a tailor for a suit of clothes. He measured me this way and that—arms, legs, waist, chest, shoulders, and so on.

I really had very little money to spend, so I chose a piece of cloth that would make a suit for a small price. Now even in those days, when money stretched further than it does today, what I paid wouldn't buy much of a suit.

I didn't know that. Learning the truth was part of my education.

For when the suit was finished and I tried it on, I knew instantly what a mistake I had made. It looked cheap from the first moment.

However, I hid my pride and told the tailor it was wonderful and how pleased I was with the suit. You know, we all hate to admit we've been foolish.

A week or so later the pants began to bag at the knees. No amount of pressing could keep a crease. Buttons began to come off. Seams popped. Holes appeared in the pockets. I was ashamed to wear the thing, but I was in no financial condition to run out and get another, better one. I knew that I should have paid a few dollars more so that I could be proud of what I was wearing. But it was too late.

That cheap suit taught me a valuable lesson—a lesson worth much more than the few precious dollars I sank into that miserable piece of cloth. I learned this: *You can't get something for nothing.*

No skilled pianist, teacher, minister, salesman, farmer, baseball

22

player, housewife, mechanic, or any other craftsman becomes good at his job without effort. God did give us our brains and bodies. They cost us nothing. But their proper use doesn't come easy.

Somebody once asked a great comedian what made him so funny. He replied: "Work, work, work." Even making people laugh is work, if you do it for a living.

Jesus Christ lived the greatest life the world ever saw, before or since. Because he is the chosen Son of God, you might think his perfect, spotless character came without effort. Not so. Not even Jesus got something for nothing.

Read the four Gospels. There you find how he suffered, worked, sweated, got tired like the rest of us, grew weary and discouraged, made enemies when he did his duty, had friends desert him when he needed them most, and finally had to die that we might be saved. The salvation of mankind was achieved at great cost to the greatest man who ever lived.

Nothing good comes cheaply. Read our history, especially American history. Every advance in government, science, and religion has been made because *somebody paid the price*.

In your own life remember: *You can't get something for nothing!*

Whether you are buying a suit or preparing for a career, you must pay the right price. Making a fine Christian home, building a strong Christian character, serving the world according to your conscience—all these goals require a price. You get what you pay *for*. And you pay *for* what you get. Ask God to help you pay whatever price his way for you requires.

11. It's Easy to Destroy but Hard to Build

AN OLD CHINESE PROVERB GOES SOMETHING LIKE THIS: "ANY FOOL CAN throw a stone down a well, but it takes a wise man to get it out!" Which is one way of saying that anybody can tear down, but it's difficult to build up.

Not many years ago this happened: A small boy of four wanted to ride his older sister's tricycle. He had taken his turn, but he wanted another, and before the others had had their turns.

Because he couldn't have his way, he got very, very peevish and angry. And he plotted revenge, real revenge.

He sat quietly on the ground right near where his sister would ride next. Down the hill she came, pumping the pedals as fast as she could. Suddenly her small brother pulled a stick from behind his back and thrust it through the front wheel spokes.

Tear, crash, pop! And in two seconds the front wheel was ruined forever, half the spokes ripped out. What had been a nice, new tricycle seconds before was now just useless junk. Needless to say, this boy got what he needed.

But no amount of punishment could bring back the tricycle. All the great skill which went into its construction was nothing compared to the angry thrust of one four-year-old boy. All the risk and daring of the coal miners who dug coal to melt the iron going into the tricycle. All the skill of steelworkers, the great experience of men who made the rubber tires, the education of men who designed the machine—its seat, springs, handlebars, wheels, and other parts. This four-year-old kid tore up their work in a split second.

The old nursery rhyme about Humpty Dumpty illustrates this

lesson so well. All the king's horses and all the king's men literally can't put an egg back together again.

So many things in this life are hard to build and easy to destroy. For example, reputation and character.

You may work hard to be known as honest and reliable. Yet, somebody can destroy or seriously damage your reputation by a few careless or spiteful remarks. The tongue, if unwisely used, is a most dangerous weapon. Never use it to destroy anybody's character.

Will you be a builder or destroyer in your life?

Will you help build up your church, your school, your scout troop, your community? Or, will you help tear them down by plain laziness or the wrong kind of talk?

The world needs builders. Not only builders of buildings, highways, factories, and bridges, but it also needs character-builders. It needs men and women who'll plan and put up great lives— their own and others.

Make up your mind now. Will you tear down or build up?

History's great people are those who built.

12. Digging Foundations for Large Buildings

WHAT'S UNDERNEATH THE TOWERING SKYSCRAPERS OF NEW YORK City? Rock, of course. Nothing else would hold up such structures.

Just how these buildings are put up is a fascinating story in itself. For truth is always more interesting than fiction. And often more unbelievable.

When a contractor signs a contract to erect one of these tall buildings, he calls in a specialist firm that specializes in constructing foundations. What does he do? Why, he puts in the foundation, then turns the job back over to the original contractor, who will build everything above the ground level.

The foundation contractor goes by very carefully drawn plans. How many pounds will this beam bear? What stress will such and such concrete pile take? What proportions of sand, water, and cement must be mixed into the concrete? How deep at such-and-such a spot must he drill before he strikes bedrock? Nothing less will bear the millions of pounds of steel and stone soaring forty, fifty, and sixty stories high.

The answers to all these and hundreds of other questions are in the blueprints and specifications drawn up by the architects who planned the building. Each rivet, each piling hole, each steel beam, each plate, girder, and brace have been carefully planned.

Such is the building of skyscraper foundations. Nothing is left to chance. For a towering building demands a strong substructure on which to stand.

We can learn lasting lessons from these foundation-builders. For, like a beautiful, strong building, which resists the winds and rains, a strong Christian life demands a good foundation.

One of Jesus' greatest parables is the story of two men who built houses—one on sand and the other on rock. Needless to say, the first collapsed when the winds came and the rains fell, while the second stood as sturdy as the rock underneath.

An adult life can be no stronger than the foundation laid in the days of youth. If you are thrifty, industrious, unselfish, helpful, worshipful, and kind now—you'll probably be just that kind of person thirty years or fifty years hence. The opposite is true. If you are rude, inconsiderate, ungrateful, and self-seeking now, the chances are that you'll be a very unattractive person in middle age.

Yes, we can change later. But it's awfully hard to change your character when you're grown. The worst of it is—the older you get, the surer you become that you don't need to change. *Now,* this minute, this day, this week—is the time to build your life's foundation.

How many men wish they could establish new habits of work. But years and years of the wrong habits can't be easily changed. *Now* is the time to build that strong, Christian, attractive personality you want to be some day. Build a strong foundation and the building will somehow take care of itself. Believe it or not, that's the truth.

13. The Man Who Could See Only Money

ONCE THERE WAS A MAN WITH A STRANGE EYE DISEASE. WHEN HE was about fifty years old, his eyes began to behave very peculiarly.

Perhaps you have heard of persons who saw spots or specks in front of their eyes. This man's trouble was similar. Only, instead of seeing spots, he saw dollar marks. No matter where he looked, his vision was cluttered up by images of large dollar signs in each eye.

At first he only saw this large "S" sign with two lines through the middle when he was at his place of business. Then he saw it whenever he looked at a customer, then when he looked at the outdoor scenery. Finally, he couldn't even look at his wife's face without seeing a large dollar sign right in the middle of her face.

It was disconcerting, to say the least. Furthermore, it was dangerous. He even found it difficult to read the markers along the highway or to tell whether a traffic light was red or green.

He had always thought of the dollar sign as the most pleasing of all insignia, especially when written in black ink. Now he positively hated it. Yet he couldn't escape the sight of it. The big double-crossed "S" was the last thing he saw at night and the first picture to cross his vision in the morning. He even dreamed of it in bed.

Before he told anybody about his affliction, he went to the dime store and tried the most expensive spectacles on the counter. They brought no relief.

Then he sought help from the local eye doctor. He didn't tell the doctor what was really the matter but complained of "eye-strain." The doctor fitted him with fine-looking horn-rimmed glasses, but these, too, did him no good. In fact, just thinking of what the glasses cost made his affliction worse than ever. Finally, his wife, who was alarmed over his frequent headaches, made an appointment for him with a famous city specialist.

As they neared the specialist's office, his eyes throbbed with pain. Dollar signs literally danced before his eyes, so worried was he about what the doctor might charge him. He could barely make out the letters on the medical diploma which hung in the waiting room.

The specialist examined him thoroughly, checking him from head to toe. After the examination he asked Mr. Jones, for that was his name, many questions about his personal and business life. Mr. Jones was not used to being treated so, and declared that he came for a check on his eyes, not a mental examination.

The physician turned and looked out the window a long time. Then he faced Mr. Jones and said: "Mr. Jones, I could fit you with eyeglasses and charge you fifty dollars, but you wouldn't be helped in the least. The trouble isn't in your eyes at all, but in your general system. My prescription is most unusual. You can follow it if you want. That's up to you. Or you can try another specialist. But I guarantee that you will lose your entire vision unless you take my advice!"

Mr. Jones pondered. He knew this man was telling the truth, for he was the greatest eye specialist in the country. He nodded to the doctor.

"What is it? I'll do anything to see like I once did. Why, this morning I couldn't see my son's face at breakfast. Only a large dollar sign perched on his neck."

When the doctor told him his prescription, Mr. Jones was the angriest man you ever saw. He wouldn't *do* such a crazy thing! What would become of his business? He didn't have time for such tomfoolery. He came for medical advice, not sermons, he said. The doctor told him he was finding it hard nowadays not to give both.

Well, Mr. Jones did try. Considering his stubborn nature, he tried exceedingly hard. He took a six-months vacation from his business and raised his assistant's salary one-third for him to run his affairs during his absence.

Then he took a tour of slums in nearby cities, visiting around in poor homes with social workers, ministers, priests, and others whom society pays to deal with people down on their luck.

He saw crippled men who were injured years before in accidents and whose wives worked hard to supplement their small pensions. He saw families where the father was serving a prison term. He saw how ashamed their children were and how the wives worked long hours to provide them with decent clothing and food.

He went with the public health nurse and saw children who were losing their teeth because of poor diets. He saw young mothers who looked old at thirty from hard work and too many children.

Mr. Jones was terribly saddened and yet angry when he visited slums where people were crammed together in horrible tenements, whole families living in one room. His conscience burned with the recollection that his own minister had described this very place when appealing for mission money, and that he, Mr. Jones, had refused to give.

He saw children under five playing ball in the dirty streets, many blocks away from a public playground. He wanted to know how any city could be so shortsighted as to allow this condition to exist. He visited camps where lived migrant workers who pick the beans, apples, grapes, and other crops. There he saw many children who never attended any school or church because their parents moved so frequently. Their pale little faces haunted him.

His doctor's prescription took him to the "home" of his wife's cleaning woman. He wondered how she could possibly face such quarters after a day of work in his own fine home. Yet, she always seemed cheerful enough.

Mr. Jones entered the home of one of his own employees, a mild fellow named Nelson. He saw how Nelson's children loved their father, especially the six-year-old boy in bed with rheumatic fever. Mr. Jones vaguely remembered hearing about the child's illness, but he had never interested himself in his employees' personal affairs. Now, the boy's face, full of innocence and intelligence like a faun's, replaced the dollar signs before his eyes. For the first time in years Mr. Jones shed tears. Two great big salty drops ran down his cheeks, followed by others. He told the Nelsons he had a cold and quickly departed.

Next morning at breakfast he saw his wife clearly for the first time in months. To tell the truth, he hadn't given her a good look in years, anyway. He had been too busy making money. Now he saw with pride how much she resembled the bride of twenty-five years ago.

He began to see other people's faces clearly too. Instead of dollar signs atop their necks, he saw their eyes, ears, noses—the entire face. He saw them as people.

When he finally returned to his business, he was a cured man, and a changed one. Some of his employees thought the old man "is going batty," but they soon decided it was a pleasant form of insanity and much nicer in every way than whatever bothered him before. When a clerk made a bookkeeping mistake, he didn't rage like he did in the old days, but gave a hearty laugh and told them to straighten it out somehow or "charge it to profit and loss." However, the business seemed to gain all the time, despite his new careless attitude toward money. In fact, business was so good, he raised every employee's wages.

He sent the Nelson boy to the best medical specialist. Within a short time the child was much better.

He was such a changed man that many of his business friends asked him the secret of his new-found health. Some of them complained to him: "I keep seeing funny things in front of my eyes. . . ."

Then Mr. Jones would say with the gusto of somebody who has made a great discovery: "I know just the man for you!"

14. Somebody Important Is Thinking of You

IF A FRIEND SHOULD TELL YOU THAT THE PRESIDENT OF THE UNITED States thinks about you every day, you'd have good reason to laugh. For, with all his many duties, how could he even think of a few hundred people daily, much less the millions of American citizens who make up our land?

Just the same, all of us would be terribly flattered if the president did think of us or inquire about our welfare.

The fact is, somebody much more important than the president *is* thinking about you, and me, and all of us, and not just once a day, but *all* day *every* day.

This person is God. Every minute, every hour, every morning, noon, and night—God is actually watching over us.

How does he do this with more than two and a half billion of his human children spread over the earth? It works like this. Human parents who have one child give that child all their attention. Yet, parents who have two, three, five, ten, or twelve children seem to love each one as much as the other parents love their one. Now God can think not just about one, two, ten, a hundred, thousand, million, or billion! He keeps each one of us in mind all the time.

Right now, this very moment, he is thinking of you. But not *just you,* or even me, as important as we think we are. God is also thinking of the Chinese babies, the African old people, the Swedish boys, the French girls, the Canadian millionaires, and the poorest peasants of South America.

To be exact, God is thinking about and watching over every man, woman, boy, and girl in the whole world. Rich and poor, good and bad, young, old and middle aged, black, white, brown, red, and yellow—the whole vast population that makes up the human race—he's looking at each one separately.

He knows their problems. He helps them when they ask for his assistance. He listens to their troubles. He is glad when they obey him and sad when they disobey. So, this very important Person, our heavenly Father, *is* thinking about you all the time, even this very minute.

Jesus told us that not a sparrow falls to the ground without God knowing it. God knows how many hairs you have on your head, even if you don't. He knows how many million blood vessels—veins and arteries—you have in your body.

How and why does he think about us? First of all, he is God and can do such vast and incredible acts that human beings can't begin to imagine. God is without limit in his power.

Next, he keeps us in mind because he loves us. We are his children. He never forgets us for one instant, even though we may forget him.

When you say your prayers tonight, remember that God is listening, ready and anxious to hear. He'll be thinking of you then, just as he is this very moment. This very important Person will never forget any of us.

15. Why a Mountain Stream Is Beautiful

WHY IS A MOUNTAIN STREAM ONE OF NATURE'S LOVELIEST SIGHTS? And so interesting?

Some say "because it's flowing." Yes, but that's only part of the answer, for many streams that flow rapidly are not half so fascinating as the brook that tumbles down a mountainside.

The mountain stream is interesting because of the obstacles it encounters on its rush to the sea. Mainly rocks, these obstacles create the splash, spray, gurgle, roar, and white foam which make the mountain stream man's delight.

Suppose, if you can, that the stream ran down a perfectly smooth creek or river bed—smooth on the sides and the bottom—with no curves, no big boulders in the middle, no deep pools to hold it back? We wouldn't care to look at it long.

The things that get in its way make it interesting. But that's only half the benefit. The indescribable beauty we can see.

Another result of these obstacles we see only indirectly. The stream is made and kept fresh, pure and life giving because of the rocks.

We all know that a flowing stream purifies itself. A mountain stream keeps doubly fresh. Agitated constantly, swirling around the rocks, and thrown into contact with the air by waterfalls and rapids, it absorbs more than its share of oxygen.

Harmful bacteria die rapidly in such water. And fish, especially game fish such as trout, find it a perfect spot to live.

The mountain stream has a lesson for us. It is the obstacles which get in our way and seem to impede us, that make our lives interesting, beautiful, and worth while. In reading biographies of great men, which we should all do as young people, we find the most interesting phase of their lives to be the early days of struggle, deprivation, and hardship.

The dullest kind of life possible is one devoid of struggle. Take away the discipline of doing without, of working for what we want, of suffering for a great cause, and you create a dull, childish, uninteresting personality. Many boys and girls have been spoiled by having everything their own way.

God could have made us like a spider, the creature that has nothing to learn. The spider is born with completely developed instincts. It knows, the second it pops out of its tiny egg, just how to build a perfect spider web, catch flies, and be a model spider.

Human beings are not so. We must struggle, struggle, struggle, to become grown-up, mature children of God. And it is the obstacles we encounter and conquer that make us better people.

If you learn the mountain stream's complete lesson, you'll even have fun while overcoming handicaps. It sings, hums, roars, and laughs its way around the rocks. It actually seems to have fun. And *your* most interesting experiences in life will be *overcoming obstacles*. Life is dull without a struggle against odds. It is made rich by exertion.

16. *Lessons from the Milkweed*

NATURE LITERALLY CRIES OUT WITH GREAT MORAL TRUTHS—IF we stop long enough to listen.

For example, who'd ever think that the milkweed teaches us the lesson of patience and perseverance? Actually, it's one of our most interesting American plants.

In the first place, it grows almost everywhere—North, South, East, and West. Roadsides, pastures, meadows, and field. If you cut it down, it comes right back. Cut it down twice, three times, or four—the milkweed puts out new shoots and miraculously makes up for lost time, barely getting its silky, wind-borne seeds out by frost.

During the war milkweed down was used in life preservers. Its whitish fluid, which oozes out when cut, contains natural rubber.

This ordinary plant teaches us patience by the way it works to reproduce itself. Follow the seeds as they float along so daintily, driven by autumn winds.

A few land in the roadside ditch and are soon covered with mud. They will never sprout. Some are eaten by birds and field mice. Perhaps a few dozen land on leaves, too far removed from the ground to send down roots. Some are caught in the pod and never "get off ground," so to speak. Others go high and wide to unknown destinations.

In the spring just a few out of the hundreds of lovely seeds actually get started. Grazing cows bite most of these or pull them up by the roots. Yet, to reproduce one, two, or three milkweed plants, the parent weed of last year expended hundreds, or even thousands, of seeds. So lavish is nature in its expenditure. So patient is God.

If somebody should ask us, "Will you try 789 times in order to succeed just once?" the answer could easily be *no*. Nature finds it necessary to expend gigantic efforts for success.

The oyster lays millions of eggs annually to reproduce itself. Every fall the maple tree sheds untold thousands of seeds with propeller-like attachments. They twist and spiral to the ground. All this to produce one or two maple saplings.

Some of us think, like the disciple Peter, that forgiving people seven times is enough. Jesus told Peter, "Not seven, but seventy times seven!" He really meant forgive an endless number of times, as our heavenly Father forgives us without ceasing.

Were God as impatient with us as we are with one another, he surely would have destroyed the human race long ago. What great forbearance he possesses! What patience it must take to be the Father of the whole human race!

The milkweed sends out its numberless seeds on wings of wind to keep the milkweed race going. Every species of plant or animal must give of itself, just to stay alive.

To develop into mature, Godlike men and women, boys and girls, we need to become more patient. Look around and you'll see his great patience displayed everywhere.

17. Our Most Wonderful Tool —Hands

WHAT IS THE MOST WONDERFUL TOOL IN THE WORLD? IS IT A monkey wrench, a pair of pliers, a hammer, saw, or one of those giant automatic machines which manufacture our radios, automobiles, and toys?

No, the most wonderful tool in the world is the oldest one we have—the human hand. Yes, the human hand, old as mankind itself. And even more wonderful is the fact that we're born with this marvelous tool.

A tool is an instrument with which we make something. It isn't just for show or ornament, however lovely it might be. A hammer is made for driving nails; a saw, for cutting wood. Other tools also do just one, two, or several things. But the human hand is almost without limit in the number of jobs it can perform.

We use our hands to pick up food, tie shoelaces, drive cars, write letters, bake bread, turn pages in a book—well, in fact, you could go on all day listing what the human hand does.

If you list all the items and articles you use and see every day, every one of these except the ground and air itself was made by the human hand.

How does God intend for us to use these two marvelous tools he gave us—the most marvelous in the world? First, let's list a few of the *wrong* ways.

Some people use their hands to hit others. They double up this fine tool into fists—hard, round weapons. Or, they take up man-made weapons in their hands, such as guns, swords, and bombs to injure and kill. We know that God never intended that our hands be weapons or that they hold weapons, for Jesus told us "to love one another."

Other people use their hands to grab. They grab what belongs to their neighbor. When they can't get what they want by force, they use their hands to steal.

Some people use their hands to wring. That is, they just sit around being sad, rubbing one hand on the other while saying: "Oh, too bad. I wish I could do something but I can't!"

How did Jesus use his hands? Well, he didn't use them to hit, grab, or wring. First, being a carpenter, he used them for many years to build useful articles of peace. He made chairs, tables, ox yokes, rake handles, and the like.

When he stopped his carpentry work for his great ministry, he used his strong, firm, gentle hands to help people.

He touched the blind, and they saw. He laid his hands on the cripple, and they walked. He gave hungry people bread, and they went away satisfied. He put his two precious hands on the sick, and they were made well.

Finally, he carried his own cross with his two strong hands—those hands which were nailed to the wood by the cruel soldiers.

God wants us to use our hands to help. This most marvelous tool, given by him, can be a force for good or an instrument of evil. Which will it be? This is for *us* to decide.

18. The World's Most Intricate Machine

IF THE HAND IS NATURE'S MOST WONDERFUL TOOL, THEN WHAT IS her most wonderful machine?

Again, it is a God-given one. It comes fully equipped, ready for operation, and with a lifetime guarantee. We pay literally nothing for it, and its maintenance cost is very low. Only now and then does it need repairs, and these repairs are often necessary only because of our own neglect or abuse.

This machine is *the human body,* of which the hand is a small but essential part.

No human being could construct such an intricate machine, each part fitted and co-ordinated with the rest. Only with a great knowledge of anatomy, can we truly appreciate how truly perfect God created this human body of ours.

I tell my hand to move, to operate the typewriter, to open the door, to pick up a pencil, and it obeys without question. I speak no words. In some mysterious fashion the command is communicated to the fingers, thumb, wrist, forearm, upper arm, and shoulder. Each of these parts must be co-ordinated with the rest.

Is the message sent by electric impulses or by some kind of radio waves from the brain? Some scientists think the latter.

I eat a candy bar. I chew and swallow, and then forget it. But my body doesn't. Instantly my digestive organs go into action, breaking the food down into usable chemical compounds, which are sent through an amazing series of chemical processes, converting the candy into a form my cells and tissues can use. The circulatory system, or the blood stream, then takes over and transports these transformed chemicals to all parts of the body.

38

Not to waste any motion, the blood brings back waste material on its way back, depositing these wastes in the proper places.

God gave us tissue we call muscle, which provides power to move the body and to do its internal work. He provided a framework of bone that we call the skeleton.

Each part and system of the body is designed to assist and work with every other part. No man-made machine can possibly compare with it.

Actually, we ourselves don't own this machine. We merely occupy it until it's worn out. God lets us use it, true. But the way we use it greatly concerns him.

He wants it used for good purposes, just as Jesus Christ, when on earth, went about "doing good" with his body. God wants us to use our bodies for his glory and for the service of our fellow men.

Let's use this world's most marvelous machine for him.

19. The Secret of Having Friends

THIS IS A SECRET MANY PEOPLE LEARN. NOT THAT IT'S SO HARD. Or, that it's any real secret. The answer has been public property for thousands of years. But, like so many other great truths that cost nothing and pay huge dividends, this secret of how to have friends eludes millions of people even today.

We all want friends. If we say we don't, we're not telling the truth. Often those who want them most have the fewest friends. They simply don't know how to attract them.

Here's how to have friends: *The way to have a friend is to be a friend.* Just that simple.

Naturally, being nice looking, good at sports, smart, well dressed, and all that, does help. Some of us are gifted. We attract people like honey attracts flies. Other individuals seem to gravitate toward us, pulled by that mysterious force we call "personality."

This is not written for such people. They need little help in making friends.

But suppose you're *not* one of these fortunates. Suppose you're one of those doing well to have just one friend. And when that one moves away or you move, you're left without any. Or, suppose you're so timid and shy other boys and girls think you're really unfriendly and so leave you alone. This happens all the time. In such a case, *you* must take action. For you can change more easily than you can change the world.

If you want friends, be a friend. And be friendly. Force yourself to smile and speak to others, even when you're afraid inside you won't be answered. Go out of your way to be helpful, even though you're snubbed once in a while.

If you see some boy or girl who, like yourself, is lonely, be extra courteous and friendly with them. You'd be surprised at how many there are who're afraid inside too.

Then join some group or organization in school or church, where you can mix and mingle with others your own age. Also, develop some skill or interest or hobby that will give you a talking subject with other people. I know one boy whose hobby of stamp-collecting gives him an excellent topic of discussion with people, including adults.

Develop your athletic ability all you can. This will give you confidence in many ways not connected with athletics. Any boy or girl not physically handicapped or cripple can become good in some sport, if they try hard enough. Once having developed your skill, you can then teach others or give them that assistance you wanted so badly not long ago.

There are a thousand-and-one ways to have friends, but they all boil down to this: *Be friendly; be a friend.*

Jesus Christ was a friend, even to those who hated him. Today he has millions of faithful friends all over the earth, friends who would die for him. Study his methods and you'll have friends too.

20. Climbing a Mountain and Living a Life

A FEW YEARS AGO TWO YOUNG MEN STOOD AT THE FOOT OF Mount Madison in the Presidential Range of the White Mountains of New Hampshire. The White Mountains are the highest mountains in the Northeast, towering high above the tree line. On their tops not even small shrubs grow. Nothing but moss and grasses.

These two youths had on their backs heavy packs of food and blankets. Their job was to open up the hut used during the summer by hikers, on top of Mount Madison. They were to pack in supplies.

One young man, whom we shall call Jim, told the other, who had never packed so heavy a load up a mountainside: "Just keep going. Put one foot in front of the other, until you get there. No matter how tired you get, keep going! One step at a time, and you'll get there in about four hours."

The other young man did just that, until he thought he couldn't make it another inch. Somewhere up ahead, he knew, was the hut. But he was so tired, that he doubted he'd ever get there. Step, step, step; up, up, up.

Finally, when the hut came into view, he simply flopped on the ground. He'd made it! And how? By taking one step at a time.

Life is like that. Somewhere up ahead is a wonderful destination. We'll call this destination *what you want to be and do*. It's so far!

You've never been there, naturally. And it looks so far up and so far away you don't think you ever will.

But you can be like the mountain climber. Set your goal, one that really exists and that you can attain. Not like something in a movie or TV program, where success, riches, and fame just seem to drop into one's lap. That happens to very few people, and mostly in stories.

Whatever your goal is, it's likely to be gained as we climb a mountain—by taking one step at a time. By living each day to the fullest, doing each task the best we can as it comes to us, accepting each challenge with everything we've got.

Some boys and girls think daydreaming will bring them what they want. Dreams are necessary. It takes the dreamer, the thinker, to imagine what's ahead.

But mere dreams and thoughts are not enough. Tremendous effort, patience, and endurance move us ahead, one step at a time.

Life is very peculiar in this respect—you cannot hurry the time. Days cannot be lengthened or shortened. But you can make the most of each day, taking each one as it comes, and not worrying about the days ahead. If this one is lived well, those in the future will be better too.

Climbing a mountain or living a life—take each step, one at a time. There's no short cut in either.

21. How Your Habits Grow

BEFORE ME, AS I WRITE, SITS A JAR OF FINE WHITE POWDER, MUCH like flour in appearance. In fact, you couldn't tell the difference.

This powder is called *plaster of Paris*. If you've ever had a broken bone and the doctor wrapped your limb in a cloth strip covered with a whitish looking substance, then you know what plaster of Paris is. Within a few moments after it has been moistened, it sets into a rocklike substance that cannot be bent. In fact, considerable strength is required to break it.

Habits, both good and bad, are somewhat like plaster of Paris. Once formed and rigidly set, it requires a strong person— strong of character, that is—to break them. This applies to our physical, mental, and spiritual habits.

For example, when I was a junior in high school, I took a course in typewriting. Not as wise as I thought I was, I tried for speed instead of accuracy, just the opposite of what the typing teacher advised. In my haste, I formed the habit of making certain errors. Today, twenty-five years later, I still make these mistakes. How many thousand times I have misspelled certain words would be hard to estimate. All because of habits formed when I was fifteen.

One lad I know played poor basketball. He could throw, but he couldn't hold the ball when it was thrown to him. Finally, his coach noticed that he held his hands in a poor position for catching. He made the boy catch several thousand times, until his hands automatically assumed the correct position. The boy went on then to make the team, something he'd never have been able to do with his old habit.

One girl I know puts her homework off until late at night or the next morning. Result—she's either too sleepy or too hurried to do good work. Unless she corrects herself, she'll go through life doing poor work, far below her real ability.

The Rockefeller family is known the world over for its generosity. An accident? Not at all. The original Rockefeller millionaire, John D. Sr., made it a practice to give one tenth of his income to his church. As a boy, making fifty cents a week, he gave a nickel. As his income grew, so did his donations. Finally, he established huge foundations, or organizations, to give away his money in a sensible way.

If you form the right spiritual habits now, some day you'll be the kind of person you want to be. Frequent prayers, daily Bible-reading, regular attendance at church, the attitude of humility, the spirit of friendship and love for others, the feeling of sympathy toward the less fortunate—all these spiritual habits you are forming now, or you aren't. One or the other.

Our lives are like the plaster of Paris. Once formed, they are very hard to change. It works either way. Develop good, Godly, Christlike habits and attitudes, and you'll be a strong character when you're grown. And now is the time to begin.

22. *That Amazing Calculator Under Your Hat*

No MATTER WHAT WONDERFUL INVENTIONS MAN MAY CONCOCT, God always goes him one better. If we think we've done great things, we usually find that God has been there first. We're only second-rate imitators.

Take this matter of the amazing calculating machines our physicists are now inventing. In less than a second they solve mathematical problems that would baffle even the smartest professors for weeks. Or they store up information and rattle it off on cards or tape whenever you request it.

But each of us possesses a far more amazing calculating machine. We were born fully equipped with it. No wires, no transistors or tubes, no electric power lines, nothing to go wrong. It comes fully protected in a bony container we call our "skull." Right, you guessed it—the human brain.

No, it can't solve some of those higher math problems. It could if we persisted and learned enough math. But it is an all-round, general-purpose machine, the most amazing, mysterious, and truly wonderful creation on earth. It weighs only a pound or so. But look what it has done.

44

With this God-given human brain, man designed and made the pyramids of Egypt. He dug the Panama Canal. He has conquered deadly diseases and will conquer more. He has split atoms and put them back together again. He has designed, made, and operated a telescope that will explore universes billions of miles away. He has taken various sounds, put them together, and produced what we call music. He "stores" or puts away this music on records or tape, so that we can reproduce it at any time we desire.

He makes airplanes that fly higher and faster than any bird, taking hundreds of people through the sky. Some day, possibly within your lifetime, man will fly to the moon and back. You might even go yourself.

He creates huge ships which sail the oceans daily, bearing thousands of people. All these miracles are products of the God-given brain.

With this brain we remember. Words, scenes, pictures, sounds, smells—everything we ever saw, heard, or experienced, is stored up in our brains and can be called back. Sometimes, when we dream at night, our brains *do* bring back long-forgotten events.

We solve problems with our brains. In fact, man thinks up problems and then solves them. He even invents and constructs the complicated calculating machines we mentioned a moment ago.

We do all this, and more, at the same time using only about one-tenth of our brain power. Scientists tell us this is true—nine-tenths of our brain power goes unused. Some people we know use much, much less than others.

While doing the mental problems, our brain controls our bodies. Where and how we walk, what we eat, the words we say —all these functions are brain controlled.

God gave us this marvelous brain. He wants us to use it for his glory and mankind's benefit. *That is its real purpose.*

23. God Erases Our Mistakes —If We Want Him To

THE MODERN LEAD PENCIL IS A PERFECT EXAMPLE OF MASS PRODUC-
tion. For a nickel we can buy this amazing article assembled
from so many parts of the world. Actually, the lead pencil contains no lead. No real lead, that is. The dark part in the middle,
which makes the mark, is really graphite, a mineral composed
of carbon.

Most graphite used in American pencil factories comes from
Africa. The rubber eraser probably originates in southeast Asia.
The wood may have come from Tennessee or Oregon. The
metal band could come from any of our iron mines.

Any kindergarten pupil knows how to use the pencil. With
one end you make marks, including mistakes. With the other
end you rub out mistakes. It's that simple.

We make mistakes in life too. We say, do, and think mistakes. If they are intentional, if they are performed with a bad
motive, we call these mistakes sins. A sin is the breaking of one
of God's laws. Sin always hurts us the most, even when other
persons are injured by what we do.

For example, we may tell an ugly falsehood about a classmate.
Naturally, it damages his reputation. But we are hurt twice as
badly. If the falsehood is proved to be just that, then we are
shown to be a bearer of bad tales. Also, we feel bad about our
misdeed. Our mistakes hurt us twice.

We all make these moral mistakes. We all sin. Sometimes we
sin by *failing* to do the right thing. More people sin this way
than any other. So, we can make the mistake of doing nothing.
For example, you may see a child mistreated by an older boy
or girl. You do nothing. You know this is wrong. Or, you may

46

hear a falsehood repeated and passed on. You know it will damage an innocent individual. Yet, you do nothing. This is a sin, too, as much as if *you* had repeated the lie.

Yes, we all make these mistakes that we call sins. But there is a way to erase them from our lives. That is by asking God, our heavenly Father, to forgive us.

He will forgive if we admit or confess our sins to him, try to set right our wrongs, and if we forgive those who have wronged us. In the Lord's Prayer we pray. "And forgive us our debts, as we forgive our debtors." This means we may ask God to forgive our sins if we will forgive those who hurt us.

How does he forgive sin? We don't know. But if we can believe what Jesus Christ said, we know that God does forgive. He erases the wrongdoing from our soul. He wants us to ask his pardon. Why should we bear a heavy load of guilt in our hearts, when we can obtain forgiveness? As our sins pile up, the load inside grows heavier. Finally, it may become too heavy to bear.

Then we should say to God: "Please forgive me for my wrongs. I'm sorry for my past and will do better in the future, with your help. Please forgive me, O God!"

Murderers, bank robbers, thieves of the worst sort—all these can confess their sins to God and be forgiven.

We all have faults. We all make mistakes. But, with God's forgiveness, they can be erased. Jesus promised us that. Confess your sins to God, and he will forgive.

24. House Plans and Life Plans

ALL OVER THE UNITED STATES MEN ARE BUILDING THEIR OWN HOMES with their own hands. Last week I spent a pleasant evening with a young man who had just completed his house. He's not a carpenter, bricklayer, or contractor by trade. He's not skilled with hammer and saw. He makes his living working in a store. Yet, he's built a lovely house.

He explained to me just how he did it. Here are his words: "When I first thought of the idea, it seemed too big. Then I got some house plans from an architect. I studied them carefully. With his help I began to figure out just how I would build.

"I soon found that building a house consisted of making plans, then following them, doing each step at a time. Each plank, brick, rafter, pipe, wire, and shingle had to be put just so.

"Often I'd have to stop and study a while. Then I'd go on. In about six months, as you can see, I had built my own house."

And he does have a lovely home, one that would cost over $15,000 to buy. Yet, he built it himself.

As this young man talked, I thought: "What a good example of how to build a Christian life!"

We have an architect with time-tested plans for our lives—Jesus Christ. Jesus showed us and told us how to live.

If we take the plans he laid out for us—the wonderful acts and teachings recorded in the Gospels, we can build beautiful, strong "life houses" that will stand forever.

And how is this done? By trying to make every thought, every act, every decision, one that fits in with the master plans laid out by Jesus.

Naturally, we can't build our lives all at once, no more than you can build a house all at once. This is the mistake many young people make, thinking they can.

When my friend built his house, he first laid a strong concrete foundation. Then came the big wooden sills, then the strong uprights, then the rafters, the siding, the lathing, the plaster, and finally such items as wallpaper, and so on. Each step depended on the previous one.

So with our lives. We build each day on the previous days, weeks, months, and years. If we build each day according to

Christ's plans, we'll build a good life, one that won't be destroyed or shaken by the tests which come.

What kind of life do you want when you're grown men and women? A good, strong, happy one? Naturally.

Now's the time to start building.

25. *Our Good, Better, and Best*

ONE GREAT AMERICAN INDOOR SPORT IS LOOKING THROUGH THE HUGE mail-order catalogs that come by mail to us each spring and fall. What fun it is to turn to our favorite sections—toys, guns, sporting goods, shoes, tools, or almost anything your heart wants.

But beware of these three words when you see them describing certain articles—*good, better, and best*. And take the advice of an old hand in the catalog business, and never, never order anything but the best. No, never!

Why? Simply because nothing less than the best is good enough.

As you go through life, you'll discover this amazing fact: We usually have the choice of the *good, better, and best,* and not of the *good* and *bad*. Our failures are frequently due to choosing the second or third best, or merely the good and the better, as the mail-order catalog puts it.

Not many of us are tempted to perform truly wicked acts that would land us in reformatory school or in jail. But we are tempted to be content with ambitions, aims, and efforts that won't use half or even a tenth of our abilities. And whom do we cheat? First of all, ourselves. Then we cheat the world around us, which so badly needs the best we can give.

Did you ever hear of a Boy Scout taking this oath: "Upon my honor I promise to do *half my duty* to God and my country?" No, the real Scout goes all the way.

Once a young man approached Jesus and asked what was required of him for discipleship. Jesus replied that he must sell *all that he had* and give it to the poor. Now it is possible that if the youth had shown willingness to put Christ before his money, then Jesus would not have required this price. He was testing the young man. He failed Jesus, for he was unwilling to give up everything to be a Christian. He would give only his second best. The best cost too much, he thought.

Jesus told another story about a man who dealt in pearls. This merchant saw a beautiful pearl, one "of great price." So much did he want the best, that he sold all he had and bought it.

Another man, Jesus says, discovered a great treasure in a field. To obtain this treasure he, too, sold all he possessed and bought the field, thereby obtaining title to the treasure.

To obtain the best, happiest, most satisfying life, you must give your best to God and your fellow man. Don't hold back. Don't save half or three quarters of yourself. Strangely enough, the more we give of ourselves, the more we have left to give. The less we give, the less we have to give.

An old poem goes:

> Then give to the world the best you have,
> And the best will come back to you.[1]

Our best is usually far better than we imagine. Our bodies and brains can be far more developed than we try to make them. But the best requires a price. Pay the price, and we get the best— be it physical development, athletic achievement, scholastic achievement and rating, spiritual development, or the holding of friends.

Why do some folks lead such happy, useful lives? Are they

---

[1] Madeline Bridges, "Life's Mirror" from *The Bright Side* (New York: Noble & Noble Publishers, Inc.). Used by permission.

just lucky? No, here's the secret—they give their best, and the best comes back to them.

26. *God, the Great Designer*

USING THE EXAMPLE OF THE SNOWFLAKE TO ILLUSTRATE GOD'S inexhaustible capacity to create new and different works of beauty is almost too commonplace to mention. Yet, it is one of the best examples.

Take a piece of dark cloth, such as your coat sleeve—let a few snowflakes fall on it, and then examine them under a magnifying glass.

Each one has six sides. But each is different. Each of the billions of flakes that will fall to earth this winter will be different from the other billions. No two are alike. Include all the billions of snowflakes that have fallen since time began and that will drift to the earth in the future. No two alike, ever.

God creates each one different from all the rest, even while he is looking after the billions of stars, each as large as the sun and billions of miles from the earth.

While doing all this, he creates the leaves. Examine a few dozen tree leaves. You'll find no two exactly alike, despite their resemblance at first glance. No two will be the same. All beautifull. All exquisitely designed, as if a fairy had manufactured them with a lifetime of toil. But no two alike. Nor will they ever be.

The same principle applies throughout all nature. No two blades of grass are the same. No two crickets, or grasshoppers, or horses, pigs, flies, earthworms, or fishes. No two oysters, or eels, or birds, or snakes. In short, God makes each of his creatures different from any before or since.

When human beings manufacture articles, we make them as

much alike as we can. They're cheaper that way. But God seems to have the time and energy to make them different. We can be grateful for this fact.

For suppose he made human beings all alike. What color? What height? What weight? Blonde, brunette, or redhead? Would we all be smart or dumb? Would we all prefer chocolate, or would it be vanilla? Would our noses be long, or just a dab of flesh out front?

Human beings are all different, right down to the fingertip. You know that. The myriads of tiny ridges at our fingers' ends, on the inside, are called "fingerprints." Police capitalize on this difference and identify people absolutely and positively by these prints.

God designs us all differently. We don't just happen to be that way. He creates us with different tastes, temperaments, and abilities. How marvelously he has provided. Some of us make good carpenters; some, bricklayers; some, bakers; and some, farmers. Put our different abilities together, and we supply one another's needs.

We could go on for years listing God's creations and how each one is a lovely thing in itself. The psalmist wrote, "The heavens declare the glory of God." How true! And each new scientific discovery declares even more how truly great God is. And only he, the great Designer, is worthy of our praise and worship.

27. Keeping Your Life Pointed to God

IN ALMOST ANY DIME STORE YOU CAN BUY A COMPASS FOR TWENTY-five cents or so. And one which will work too.

A compass is nothing but a magnetized needle, freely suspended, which points to the North Magnetic Pole. If you take an ordinary sewing needle from your mother's sewing kit and magnetize it by stroking it on a magnet a few times, you can make a compass.

Take this needle, gently lay it on the surface of water covered with a film of oil so that it won't sink, and it will point north. Or, run it endwise through a short straw so that the straw will act as a "lifepreserver," and the needle will also float and point north.

The compass Christopher Columbus used on the world's greatest voyage back in 1492 was no better than the one you can buy now for a quarter. All sorts of refinements have been made since, but even the largest ship's compass does one thing mainly—it points north.

When you travel or hike through the woods, a compass, if properly used, can be of great help. Once you know the landmarks, the compass tells you what direction to go. Why? Because it always points north. From that you can figure out east, west, and south, for yourself.

As the compass directs the traveler, we all have an inside compass which points the right way on the road of life. That invisible indicator is *conscience*. Conscience tells us what is right and wrong. It points the way to God. It can, if followed, lead us to a wonderful life.

Conscience is that inner feeling that makes us feel bad when we do wrong and good when we do right. After we have told a lie or stirred up trouble against our parents or teachers, our conscience usually hurts. It tells us, "You're on the wrong track!" Contrary, it gives us a pat on the back when we go right, especially against odds.

Naturally, conscience can be ruined if we persist in wrongdoing long enough, just as a compass can be ruined by continual exposure to magnetic forces. If we *want* to stray from God, no power can prevent us.

However, we all possess an inner longing to know him, to be

with him, to do as he commands us. An invisible tie of love binds us to our heavenly Father. The upward progression of mankind indicates this.

We have helpers on this climb toward God. Parents, teachers, trusted friends, ministers, Sunday-school teachers, advisers to your Sunday youth group, a trusted employer—all these help keep us on the road.

But deep inside is the conscience. For us all, it is the final guide. If we keep it clean and untampered with, the conscience is the best guide of all. Through prayer, Bible-study, and meditation it becomes more sensitive, more certain of its Godward pointing, as each year goes by.

Keep your life pointed toward God. For that's the right direction on the road of life.

28. Don't Be Afraid to Strike Out

WHO IS GENERALLY ACKNOWLEDGED TO BE THE GREATEST BIG-LEAGUE baseball player in the game's history? Babe Ruth, naturally! Nobody denies that.

And who holds the greatest lifetime record of striking out? The same Babe Ruth!

The mighty Babe hit a total of 714 big-league home runs. In 1927 his record was sixty for the season—a mark every heavy hitter has been aiming at since.

His lifetime total of strikes-out was a whopping 1,330! In other words, he struck out almost twice as many times as he knocked home runs! When he hit 'em, he hit 'em. But when he didn't, he *really* didn't.

Babe Ruth wasn't afraid to strike out. He wasn't afraid to try. When he connected, he went places. What connection was there between his record strike-outs and his record home runs?

Just this—he wasn't afraid to strike out. He gave each swing all he had. And, by the law of averages, he connected with enough pitches to more than make up for his misses.

If there's any sin most of us are guilty of, it's the sin of not trying—of giving our second best—of failing to aim high in our lives.

Already in your life you've conquered fears and challenges that once looked insurmountable. Remember when you started to school how difficult reading and writing looked? Now you do both easily. But you still face obstacles.

Whether you conquer them or not doesn't depend so much on native ability as on your willingness to try.

The sin of omission is the sin of "not doing." Not long ago Dr. Lewis K. Sillcox, one of America's great authorities on railroads, was asked to take a hard job. At the age of seventy, most men want to avoid hard tasks. Not Dr. Sillcox. When asked to head up the financial drive for a lovely chapel at a state mental hospital, he said he would be glad to. Furthermore, he said, he considered it a duty to do all the good we can as we go along. "The sin of omission is the most frequently committed of all," he stated.

The sin of not doing. The sin of not trying. The sin of doing our second or third best. These plague us more than the excess faults. Few of us dare be truly bad. We land in jail if we are.

But no policeman will rap on our door if we do nothing. Usually nobody knows but us.

God wants us to be our best—physically, mentally, socially, and spiritually. He wants our bodies to be well developed and healthy. He wants our minds kept clear and sharp by hard thinking. He wants us to mingle freely and easily with our fellow men. He wants us to worship and love him.

To live so fully as this takes daring. We must be willing to strike out—to have people laugh at our failures as well as admire our successes.

Strangely enough, our failures teach us more than our successes ever do. Therefore, when we strike out, we are apt to learn.

Don't be afraid to strike out! Inevitably you'll hit a homerun. Babe Ruth did.

29. The Element You Can't Live Without

A FEW YEARS AGO A HISTORIC OLD MILITARY FORT ON THE SOUTHERN tip of Manhattan Island was razed. Built more than a century ago, as a watchdog for the city, its huge cannon bristled out over the harbor for decades until changing methods of warfare made it obsolete. It was called the Battery.

Then, of all things, it was changed into an aquarium. From being a military fort it was suddenly converted into the nation's outstanding showplace for fish and sea life. Giant turtles, electric eels, dogfish—all these and more—sported themselves in huge glass tanks before the interested public.

Finally, in the name of progress, the historic old Battery was demolished. When the fish were moved to another building, naturally they had to be taken from these tanks to new ones. In the process a most interesting fact came to light. The scientists in charge of the move found that these creatures died in the new water, even though it was exactly the same in every proportion as sea water. Something was lacking! What was it? Something very simple, really. That something was a small amount of water from the old tanks or from the sea itself!

What element did this tiny amount of water contain that the fishes simply *had* to have? Nobody knows, but we know that it was essential—of that we are sure.

Human beings, too, need an invisible element in order to live. No, we're thinking of air. That element we must have to live is *love*. Take away love and you take away life.

The universe is held together by love. The Bible says, "God is love."

In a way, we are like the fish in the Battery aquarium. Without one essential element—love—we cannot live. Life isn't worth living without it.

Millions of boys and girls are growing up in America without the love of their parents. They will never completely recover from this lack. Fortunate are we who were raised in homes where mother and father loved each other and their children.

People who love their work do better work than those who dislike it or who go through the motions merely to make a living. An eight-hour day seems shorter when you find your work interesting and attractive.

The subjects that you like best in school—these are the most interesting to you. Your attraction for them adds the ingredient without which school would be dull routine.

The teacher who loves his or her work does a better job than the teacher who doesn't. This principle of love runs through all of life—our work, play, courtship, marriage, politics, and even sports. The boy or girl who loves a game plays it the best.

Naturally, we can't compare these kinds of interest or attraction to the great love God has for us, but they illustrate in about one-millionth degree the love he showed when he sent Jesus Christ to the world.

God was interested in us. He cared about what happened to mankind and to each individual human being. Without his love for us the world would be a gloomy place indeed. This essential ingredient—love—is all around. Accept it from God and pass it on.

30. Is God Scientific?

THIS SOUNDS CRAZY! BUT NOT AS CRAZY AS YOU THINK AT FIRST glance. *Is God scientific?*

Is our heavenly Father, the God of the Bible, the God who sent Jesus Christ to the world, a God who understands all the mysteries of science? Is the Christian religion just for the old horse-and-buggy days, or does it fit in today?

To show how ridiculous much thinking on the subject is, let me illustrate. A group of high-school students were asked this question: *Do you think God understands radar?*

A majority answered *no*. Figure that one out!

The God who created all matter, who formulated and sustains all the laws of nature, who designed every living creature, plant and animal alike, who knows the number of atoms in the universe—this great God was thought of as less intelligent than we human beings.

Actually, we don't understand radar either. We merely use it. We have no idea as to what it is, no more than we really know what electricity is.

Is your idea of God this one: an old man with a beard who talked with people in the Bible, but who doesn't know any science? Many people have exactly this idea.

If you believe this, you're about a thousand years behind the times. Might as well believe Henry Ford never understood the Ford car. Or that Thomas Edison knew nothing of the light bulb. Or that Beethoven was ignorant of music.

Along with the crazy notion that God isn't scientific goes the absurd idea *that Jesus Christ's religion is no good in our scientific day of progress*. People reason this way: Jesus lived in a different age. He doesn't understand our problems. We know much more than he did. Therefore, his teachings do not apply to us.

Millions of people live according to this absurd doctrine. They might not admit it, but they do.

The exact opposite is the truth. *Jesus' teachings are needed more today than ever.* "Love your enemies" is terribly good advice when we can send guided missiles loaded with hydrogen bombs against one another.

The Golden Rule is far more necessary today, for we live so much closer together than did our ancestors. Also, Jesus' teachings that we should love God first and then our neighbor as ourselves certainly isn't out of date.

No, neither almighty God nor Jesus Christ, his Son, is old fashioned. They are millions of years ahead of us in every respect. *We* are unscientific, *not they*. We only understand a tiny, tiny part of God's great mysteries. He wants us to discover more and more, utilizing our minds and such instruments as the microscope, X ray, telescope, and the marvelous research tools yet to be invented.

Is God scientific? God invented, created, and maintains what we call science. Let's get over the childish notion that God's religion, revealed through Jesus Christ, doesn't apply today. The Christian faith never was stronger or more needed.

31. On Sticking Your Neck Out

HUMAN BEINGS ARE MUCH LIKE TURTLES. THE ONLY WAY WE GET ahead is by sticking our necks out.

Poor old turtle! Nature certainly put him on the spot. If he wants to go anywhere, he must put himself in a vulnerable position. With his head tucked under his shell, few natural enemies can harm him. But the moment he wants to move—what an exposed situation he's in!

Truly the human race has progressed on the backs of men who stuck their necks out! Try to find a single exception. You'll look hard and long in your history books.

You've heard the expression, "Don't stick your neck out." In other words, don't do or say anything different from what other people do or say. Otherwise you'll get into trouble.

Galileo dared proclaim the world round and the earth *not* the center of the universe, as always believed and taught before his time. For this bold statement he faced death.

Only a century ago men believed most sicknesses were caused by bad air, wicked vapors, or demons, and a thousand-and-one other silly reasons. Then a French chemist, Louis Pasteur, looking through a microscope, decided that tiny plants and animals, which we now call "germs," caused certain diseases. All the French doctors called him crazy. He stuck by his statements. Later he was proved right, of course. But, meanwhile, sticking his neck out against all the learned physicians of France was *not* very easy. Because he did, we have modern medicine, not magic.

Abraham Lincoln was advised by his political friends not to defy human slavery and make it a campaign issue against Stephen A. Douglas when they were competing for the United States Senate. Lincoln disregarded their advice and followed his own conscience. He stuck his neck out.

Yes, he was defeated in the Senate race. But his bold offensive against slavery caught the nation's eye. Here was a man not afraid to state his convictions! Our country made him president. Later, as president, he abolished slavery.

The Old Testament prophets were men who stuck their necks out. Amos, Hosea, Micah, Jeremiah, and the rest. Whatever was evil they denounced. They even called the whole nation of Israel wicked and got away with it.

In every field of human endeavor—religion, science, education, business, or government—advances are made by men who stick their necks out. Not in a foolish way, of course. But for a cause.

During your lifetime you'll be constantly faced with situations where you could remain quiet or do nothing and see an injustice done. Today whole nations of people do this, while dictators take their neighbors off to jail or concentration camps. Why? Because enough people keep their necks *in* to save them.

The world needs people who'll stick their necks out for the right. Woe to the land which possesses no such brave souls, or where there are too few!

America is a great land for neck-sticking-out. Our nation was founded by men who dared. It is full of them today. Will you be one when *you* grow up?

32. Which Is Stronger —Love or Hate?

THIS QUESTION YOU MUST ANSWER IN YOUR OWN LIFE. NOBODY CAN escape it. We live by one answer or the other.

Some of us live as if our neighbors can't be trusted or as if they're not worth wasting our time to help. We put *self* first. We regard force and might as correct instruments to settle disputes. Whoever is strongest, we say is in the right. To us, our own interests and opinions come first; nobody else's are deserving of consideration. As for God—well, he will just have to wait his turn. Meanwhile, we're too busy promoting our own affairs. We hate whatever or whoever gets in our way.

Others of us look at life differently. We regard all we have as a temporary trust from God, to be used for our fellow men. We make every decision with other people in mind. Not just our welfare, but also that of our neighbors, is important to us. We don't hate those who oppose us. We realize that we can be wrong. We put God's way before our own. This is the way of love.

Judging by the movies and TV programs, so filled with slugging matches, force and violence are about the only means man has for settling disputes. Just for interest, count the times shooting and fist fights wind up the television program you watch. Is life in your community lived like this?

Suppose Jesus had settled his disputes with those who hated him by calling down fire from heaven each time. Imagine, if you can, this scene: A gang of rogues hired by the temple priests pick up stones to kill Christ. Presto! He waves his hand. A hundred angels appear and strike the men dead. The crowd shrieks in horror and falls prostrate at Jesus' feet, worshiping him out of sheer terror.

Or, back at Nazareth, his home town, Jesus is being led to a cliff's edge. The angry mob intends to cast him down headlong onto the cruel rocks below. The Bible tells us he escaped from them. Suppose instead he had uttered a cry for help from heaven! Instantly a thousand angels appear and throw the men over to their deaths!

Had Jesus put his life and interests first, had he destroyed those who hated him, would his name mean anything to us today? Would we say: This is the Son of God? Would all mankind acknowledge him as the greatest Man who ever lived?

You know the answer. No, had Christ chosen hate instead of love, the world would remember him only as a gifted, but cruel, man.

Christ chose the way of love. However weak it appeared to his enemies, and even to some of his disciples, love proved to be stronger. For God is love. And God is all powerful.

You must decide which will rule your life—love or hate. Will you choose weak hatred that burns itself out or powerful love that increases in strength?

Don't be fooled by the big armies and air forces. They will pass. Mankind will abandon them. God's way of love and peace will prevail. *In your own life choose the winning way—the way of love!*

33. *Don't Sell Yourself Cheaply*

SUPPOSE YOU POSSESSED A DIAMOND WORTH $50,000 AND A MAN offered you a trunk full of counterfeit dollars bills for it! Your first impulse might be that of anger. Later, you might think it best to call the police and have him put in a mental hospital. No person with such a treasure would part with it, except for real money.

But believe it or not, plenty of us sell a much *more* valuable treasure for counterfeit money and worthless trinkets. We sell our souls.

A diamond is valuable, not just because it is beautiful as a jewel and able, as an industrial tool, to cut even the hardest metals, but because it has another quality that makes it a good investment. It is virtually indestructible.

A house will decay in a hundred years or more, though some last longer. With normal use, an automobile lasts only ten or fifteen years. A new suit of clothes or a new dress wears out far too soon. But a diamond will be just as bright and solid ten thousand years from now as it is today.

But, according to Jesus Christ, the divine Son of God, our souls last always, even longer than diamonds. When all the diamonds in the world have turned to dust, you and I will still be alive.

Since we will be living so long and possess souls which cannot be destroyed, isn't it absurd to sell ourselves for counterfeit money?

How can we sell our souls cheaply? We can form habits that are unbecoming to us, as children of God. We can be selfish and cause our souls to shrink up and become little. We can think of ourselves first and other people last. W can judge others harshly and think of ourselves as perfect. We can be dishonest in many little things so that when we grow up, we will be dishonest in big things.

We can take short cuts and cheat on life when we know that character is achieved only by doing the right, even when it's hard. We can be satisfied by being just as good as people around us, and often this is a low standard.

Jesus said: "Be ye therefore perfect, even as your Father which is in heaven is perfect." This obligates us to live our best always.

That soul of yours—an eternal, precious possession—can be sold for counterfeit money or trinkets. Don't. Don't sell yourself cheaply.

34. Doing What Comes Naturally

"DOING WHAT COMES NATURALLY" WAS THE SONG TITLE OF A HIT tune not many years ago.

Doing the natural thing—the act or word that comes on first impulse—isn't always the best way to act or speak. How many words we all wish we could recall—those we uttered without thinking. Or, consider the brash deeds that caused irreparable damage—done in thoughtlessness.

Hasty action can even result in our own destruction. Once an English missionary was sleeping on his back in his jungle hut. He awoke with a great feeling of heaviness on his chest and stomach. He opened his eyes slowly, just a peep, and peered out. To his horror he saw a large cobra, coiled atop his body, ready to strike!

Now the natural thing would have been to shriek in horror (or else pass out completely). But the Englishman knew that even the slightest move would mean death. Within a split second the venomous beast would sink its fangs in his face. Death would come within minutes.

Summoning his complete resources, the missionary prayed to God. Closing his eyes to avoid the snake's attention, he silently asked God to give him absolute control of his natural impulses. Not a muscle quivered. Not a tremor to reveal his terror. Within a short time the serpent slithered to the floor and outside. The missionary lived because he avoided what seemed natural.

Some of our natural impulses are good. Some aren't. Yielding to the right ones and controlling the wrong ones are part of a Christian's development.

Imagine this: You are taking a mathematics test. The teacher is out of the room. You're in trouble. You can't get four problems. Without them, you fail. By looking at your neighbor's paper, you can pass. Shall you control this natural impulse? Lack of control means you pass the math test but fail the character test.

You see a schoolmate abused, ridiculed, slighted, or made miserable and lonely through neglect. Your Christian, human impulse is to take his part. To do so means putting yourself on the spot. The natural thing in this case is to help the underdog. Yield to that impulse! You'll never be sorry.

We're all filled with natural impulses. Fortunately, more of them are good than bad. We are God's children. We have temptations aplenty. But we *are made in his image*. This means the Godlike qualities cry out for expression.

If we yielded to the temptations we have to do good, the bad ones wouldn't get in edgewise. We'd be so busy becoming Godlike, doing his will, helping our fellow man, we'd have little time for the wrong impulses.

Obey that impulse you know is the right one! Do what comes naturally—especially when you feel in your heart God wants you to.

You'll never be sorry!

35. Don't Take It Personally

IF YOU'VE EVER DRIVEN THROUGH A SNOWSTORM, SITTING ON THE front seat of an automobile, you will remember how each flake seemed to dash straight at the car. Straight at the car they flew— or so they seemed. When you stopped and got out, you found they were falling straight down, as always.

The difference was in your viewpoint.

Some people prefer to think that trouble was made for them. They take normal misfortune and setbacks personally. In school they say, "The teacher doesn't like me," and then proceed to give the teacher plenty of reason for *not* liking them. They say, "I was never good in math," and then prove this statement by neglecting their math homework. They say, "I was never a good athlete," and make this statement true by not really trying on the field or in the gym.

Later, these same people say, "I never get the breaks," and then fail to see a break when it does come their way. Or, they feel that people don't like them, and do nothing to make people like them.

They take everything personally. They remember unkind remarks and hold them against people. If rebuffed, they think the world is against them. In their jobs they're always looking for reasons why the boss doesn't like them. And they usually succeed in their search.

This attitude, in its extreme, causes some people to become mentally ill. A few enter our state mental hospitals. Others merely make life miserable for all around them.

Do you take life personally? Or do you use the handicaps, setbacks, and rebuffs as ways of learning your own weaknesses? I know one brilliant youth who failed in several jobs. He was likable, good looking, and he made friends easily. His one fault was his inability to organize his life. He hated schedules. He disliked getting up early.

Fortunately, he was smart enough to see he was his own worst enemy. Against his own nature, he set about correcting his weakness. He made himself be prompt, punctual, and early. He set schedules for himself and kept them.

Today he's happy and generally recognized as a successful man. But, how easily he could have become bitter, cynical, and a complete failure. He could have said: "God made me slipshod, and there's nothing I can do about it. The odds are against me. I never get a break!"

The bumps, rebuffs, slaps on the cheek, injustices, bad breaks, unkindnesses, misunderstandings, lack of talent in certain areas, and even deliberate cruelty from others—all these are a part of every human being's life. They're a part of growing up.

If you take them personally, as if life were sore at you, then you're in for some miserable years. But if you laugh and accept them as an expected part of life and challenges to be overcome, then you'll have a good time, no matter what comes.

Don't take normal, or even abnormal, amounts of trouble personally. Follow this rule, and you'll become a grand person.

36. *Your Money Isn't Yours*

READ THAT STATEMENT OVER AGAIN, IF YOU WISH. IT'S NO MISPRINT. Your money really isn't yours at all.

Crazy? By ordinary standards, yes.

But not by God's standards. For you see, the ordinary conception of our actually *possessing* money is wrong. We don't truly *own* anything—our clothing, homes, cars, money, not even our own bodies. We merely have the temporary use of these items. And we can't keep a single one longer than God allows us to draw breath.

Right now, while you're young, is the time to let this great truth sink in. Many individuals get it backwards. They really believe they *own* wealth. They wind up with their wealth owning *them*.

Jesus told one story after another to impress us with this truth: *We're temporary stewards,* or keepers, not final owners.

Mary makes five dollars a week baby-sitting. She's only fourteen. She buys her own clothes, goes to the movies at her own expense, and has some left over. She gives a nickel a week to the church, exactly one eightieth of her income. Is she using her—or rather, God's—money wisely? From a selfish standpoint she is correct. From a Christian standpoint she's stingy and closefisted.

Johnny makes six dollars a week working in stores after school and on Saturdays. He pledged thirty cents a week to the new Sunday-school building drive and twenty a week to church and Sunday school. He also gives to the various drives put on in his school, such as Red Cross, polio, etc.

Ralph was trained by his parents, who were selfish, never to do anything without pay. Already he's considered a poor one to ask for thankless committee work. In the back of his mind is this big question, put there by his parents: What's in it for me? Besides being a bore, he's trying to fool himself into believing he owns himself.

And believe it or not, *we don't even own ourselves.* Where did our bodies come from? God gave them to us, using our parents as his means of giving life. Ever consider that our bodies are slowly wearing out and there's no way of stopping them? Someday their physical elements will return to the earth, whence they came. Who will own them then? Certainly not us. We'll be gone.

Jesus' teachings *sound* exactly backwards. But second thought shows how right he was. We don't own a thing. It all belongs to God. Try to grasp it, and it slips through our fingers.

The wise man uses "his" possessions for God and his fellow man. That's the secret of keeping your wealth. Somebody said, "All we can take with us is what we've given away."

Jesus put it another way nearly two thousand years ago: "Lay not up for yourselves treasures upon earth, where moth and rust doth corrupt, and where thieves break through and steal; but lay up for yourselves treasures in heaven, where neither moth nor rust doth corrupt, and where thieves do not break through nor steal." So, you can take it with you, provided you don't consider your wealth yours.

Now is the time to form lifelong habits of stewardship. If you're stingy now, you'll be stingy at fifty. If you're generous now, you'll likely be generous then.

No, that money isn't yours until you give it away! Nor anything else. *Jesus gained the world by giving his life.* Don't hold back. Give yourself away. That's the real secret of Christian stewardship.

37. *How God Answers Prayer*

Does god answer prayer?

Certainly. But not in the way we ask him to every time.

Put on your imagination cap for a moment. Just imagine, if you can, that God answered every prayer exactly as we asked him.

Here are two high-school football teams; tomorrow's the big game. Suppose players, coaches, girl friends, and parents on both sides prayed for victory. Who would win? How would God answer those prayers? Put yourself in his place. What would you do?

Or, take this matter of weather. A critical big-league baseball game comes up tomorrow. The victor will go into the World Series. But all around crops are dying for lack of water. Ball fans pray for a clear day. Farmers pray for rain. Both are Christian people. What would *you* do if you were God?

Or, imagine this. Bill fidgets away in a math test, biting his nails. He knows he'll flunk. He didn't do his homework all fall. He prays and promises God he'll do better next term if he gets help right *this* minute. But can God suddenly cram Bill's head full of mathematics, just to get him off the hook? And even if he could, *should* he? Would it be good for Bill?

Ralph is strongly tempted to join the gang in a drinking spree. One boy swiped a bottle of whiskey. They're all going to get drunk, just to see how it feels. They call Ralph "chicken." He prays to God: "Please help me God, to go on home now." Should God answer Ralph's prayer? We'd all agree on that.

When I was a small boy, I promised God literally everything if he'd do certain favors for me. He never granted my prayers. If he had, he would have violated every natural law, as well as common sense.

Yes, God does answer our prayers. Many times his answers don't jibe with our prayers. So, we doubt the power of prayer.

I had very, very wise parents. They made me and my brothers and sisters work. Sometimes I doubted their justice. Some kids in town got everything from their parents. Now I see how unwise those parents were. So, God makes us work to help answer our own prayers too.

I know a sophomore in high school. He yearns for a college education. I happen to know he prays over it. *If* that boy studies hard and wins scholarships and works hard for extra money, he will finish college. Prayer will help, but it's no substitute for effort.

Sometimes God is powerless to answer even righteous prayers. Suppose he righted all injustice, healed every disease upon request, killed every dictator with bolts of lightning, released all the prisoners in Russian slave labor camps, and punished every evil thief and murderer with instant death? A lot of prayers would be answered, but we wouldn't want it that way.

Yes, he does answer our prayers, especially when we pray for the right things. He gives us strength to resist temptation, he grants us forgiveness for sins, he gives us power to love even unlovable people, he comforts us in distress.

Can we say in each instance: God answered my prayers thus and so? Not very often. "God moves in a *mysterious* way his wonders to perform." To pray takes faith that God answers prayer in his way, his time, and by his method.

Be assured of this: He does hear our prayers and he does answer them. So, pray in confidence that your prayers will be answered in a way superior to anything you can imagine.

38. *Be Yourself*

BEING YOURSELF CAN MEAN MANY KINDS OF ACTION. WHY?

Because inside all kinds of selves live. There's our worst self, our best self, our in-between self. Sometimes we do deeds or say words that make us wonder five minutes later: "Now why in the world did I do that? I just can't make any sense out of it."

Of course not. Because we're complicated creatures, far more complex than mere animals. Most animals' actions can be predicted—they act on instinct, and we've learned what to expect of these instincts.

But human beings! What a difference! Sometimes we act on instinct. The next time, from habit. The next time, from pure reason. The next, from the highest religious motive. The next, from a mixture of common sense and idealism. And so on. You see, we all have minds, our natural instincts that are built in, so to speak, our consciences that try to keep us morally straight, our bodily needs that demand satisfaction, the artificial desires that come from the world around, and other complex urges that pull us here and there. Very, very few persons act consistently from one motive only.

So, we can, if we choose, be as mean, stingy, and selfish as we please, and still be ourselves. When we steal, swear, cheat, and lie, we *are* being ourselves. But not our *best* selves. For there is another side to us—the God side. The Bible says, "God created man in his own image." What a thrilling idea: *We're like God*.

The more like him we strive to become, with his help, the more we're really our best selves. Sure, we can act like animals, but we're then being false to our heritage, no matter what excuses we give.

To be your best self, your true self, is hard, but possible. If it were impossible, do you think God would expect it of us? No, for he is a just God, not an unjust one. He expects of us no more than we can achieve.

I would like to suggest that you be:

Your best self physically. Nobody enjoys a weak, flabby, slumped-down body. Unless we're crippled by disease, there's no excuse for having such a machine to live in. You enjoy life most when you're bursting with good health. The body is the temple of the soul. It's the place we live in all our lives. Some people, who'd be ashamed to live in a shabby, unpainted, run-down house, go around in the weakest kind of bodies. Be your best self physically. Life will be better.

Your best self mentally. Scientists tell us we use less than one-tenth of our brain. Some people we know use less than that. Now is the time to sharpen your brain—to give it workouts that will pay off later. Fill your mind with great ideas, good work habits, uplifting thoughts. It takes no more storage space for good thoughts than for trashy ones. Set aside regular periods every day for study, Bible-reading, concentration, and meditation about God. Watch yourself grow mentally.

Your best self spiritually. Your soul is your most prized possession. And it's the only part of you that goes beyond the grave. What are you doing with it? Are you keeping it locked up, half-starved, poorly exercised, and forgotten? You can, you know. Simply by not using your impulses to be generous, loving, gentle, brave, and worshipful, you can shrivel up the soul, until finally it is too weak to speak up at all. Be your best self spiritually.

Yes, you can be yourself, your best self, if you pray daily for God's help. Be true to yourself, and you'll be true to him.

39. Who Are Your Heroes?

TELL ME YOUR HEROES, AND I'LL TELL YOU WHAT YOU WANT TO BE.

Tell me what you think about, and I'll tell you what you will be.

Far fetched? Not at all. For we become like the people we set up as heroes.

Nathaniel Hawthorne's story of Ernest and the "Great Stone Face" illustrates this. Ernest, a country boy, lived within sight of the Great Stone Face in New Hampshire. A legend said that some day a former resident, who resembled the huge manlikeness which towered over the lovely valley, would appear in the valley. The supposed heroes came: a great financial wizard, showering gold coins over the crowd; a famous military hero, resplendent in uniform and medals; a famous statesman, noted for his oratory; and others, noted in some field. After the shouting died down, the residents knew the man had not yet come.

Finally, they recognized the long-sought hero. It was Ernest, now grown old and wise. All his life he had looked upon the Great Stone Face until its stern, kindly visage had become his own. Its very facial characteristics were seemingly transplanted to his own countenance. *He,* Ernest, had become like the Great Stone Face.

What heroes do you worship? What is your ideal? Whom do you want to be like? Not that you can become, in fame or in national reputation, like your heroes. But their attitudes, their characters, will become yours in a mysterious fashion, as Ernest's countenance became like the Great Stone Face.

About 1940 a famous blonde movie actress wore a lock of hair over one eye. Silly? Maybe. But millions of young girls—blonde, brunette, and redheaded—started draping a lock over an eye. Ask your parents if they remember this feminine fad.

More recently a guitar-playing singer wore long sideburns. All over America, young boys in their teens told the barber not to cut off those sideburns. The fad even spread to England and Europe.

Pick out great heroes, and imitate their best qualities. Thank goodness for Florence Nightingale, the "lady with the lamp." She started the modern profession of nursing. Millions of registered nurses now imitate her skill, patience, faithfulness, and love for the suffering. She is *their* heroine and the world is a better place for their hero worship.

Thomas Alva Edison, America's greatest inventor, has inspired thousands of American boys to patient, never-flagging research and discovery. We owe him a vast debt for his discoveries. But we also owe him a greater debt for the example he set for American youth. Without him, American history would be poorer.

Jesus Christ is mankind's greatest hero. Long after others are forgotten, he will tower high as the greatest Man. Strange that one who died on the cross should be a hero. But his qualities of love, patience, forgiveness of enemies, doing good, trust in God, faith in us, and devotion to the right are the qualities we know are worth living for and dying for.

If you make him your hero, your life will be worth living. Study his life in the four Gospels. Read how, even in death, he conquered his enemies. Learn how he forgave those who killed him.

His is the greatest life ever lived. He is the greatest hero of them all. Imitate him, and your life will be great too.

40. *Don't Be Ashamed of Your Finer Feelings*

HAVE YOU EVER WONDERED WHY SO MANY OF US ARE ASHAMED OF letting others know that we have inner feelings of generosity, tenderness, love for beauty, and the many other feelings that we know are right?

For it is a fact—many of us are anxious to hide our highest ideals. Especially men and boys. And even women and girls.

Many times on the playground or on the way home from school, boys join in teasing some weaker fellow, or somebody dressed differently, or a boy with skin of another color. Girls join in pointing out some poorer girl, not dressed as well as they. Or they simply ignore her and leave her without friends or companions.

Why does this happen? Not because we are all so bad. No, that's not the reason at all.

The reason is this: Many of us are afraid to reveal that we have sympathy, compassion, pity, or feeling for the underdog. We had rather have our friends believe we're tough, inside and out.

Once when Albert Schweitzer, the great missionary doctor, was a boy, he went on a bird-hunting expedition with other boys. Inside he was deeply troubled. He didn't want to shoot the birds. He felt very sorry for them. He loved their lovely songs. Also, he felt that they deserved to live, just as much as he did. Still, he trudged along with the other fellows.

Just as they were about to shoot, the church bell started ringing. The sound brought, in a flash, all the great ideas he had learned in church. Now he knew what he must do. Without any more hesitation or indecision he made all the noise he could. The birds flew away. For a while, at least, they were safe.

Only a boy can appreciate what courage was required for young Albert Schweitzer to do this simple act. For, we can imagine what ridicule was heaped on him by his companions who had their guns loaded, cocked, and aimed, ready to shoot.

Years later the same Albert Schweitzer, now a famous scholar, teacher, preacher, and musician, revealed his inner feelings again; and again people called him crazy. He felt badly that his own white race had been so cruel to the African Negro. What could he do to make up for this cruelty? He decided to become a medical missionary. What? His friends asked. Give up a great career for colored people thousands of miles away? Certainly Albert was out of his mind!

But inside he knew what was right for him. He proceeded according to his inner feelings. He was not ashamed to let the world know just how he felt.

If you are brave enough to reveal your finest and highest thoughts, you'll have a pleasant surprise. All around people will say, "That's exactly how I feel, too, only I didn't know anybody else felt the same!"

A verse in Genesis tells us: "God created man in his own image." By this we know that all his children are essentially the same. Yes, there's bad aplenty in us all. Some seem mostly bad. But in every human being there is more good than we see on the surface.

We Christian folk must be leaders in showing our finer points. Oh, not in the boasting sense, but in the many, many opportunities, which we confront every day, to respond to God.

41. New Frontiers to Conquer

OUR FAVORITE MOVIES AND TELEVISION SHOWS ARE STILL PICTURES about the Old West and the pioneer days, aren't they? Everybody—young and old—seems to like them best.

Why? That's hard to say. Some like their historical aspects. Some like the frontier. Frontier days are always exciting. Nothing in the old frontier times was settled or stable. Few laws existed. The few they had were poorly enforced. Excitement and danger were never far away.

You might think, as I once did, that frontier days are gone forever. Yes, the West is settled, the stagecoaches rattle along only in shows and museums, the land is fenced in, and the six-shooters no longer shoot. Boot Hill hasn't seen a funeral in a long, long time.

But the frontiers aren't closed. In fact, today we have more frontiers than ever. Only they're a different kind. They're harder, more dangerous ones.

America isn't through growing. One look at the newspapers proves that. Right now we're fighting a nationwide battle to destroy segregation of people by color. We've had this frontier for many years. It will be here a long time. Just recently in the South it took a courageous Negro to ride wherever there was a seat on a public bus. At present America is on the frontier called "the right to live where we choose, regardless of our color." We're fighting for equality in the real-estate business—which means that a colored person can buy a home wherever he can afford to pay for it.

All around mankind is trying to settle the hardest, toughest frontier of them all. That frontier is "world peace." The crazy part is that we can't use guns to settle it. We're trying desperately hard to settle it without guns—just the opposite of the wild-west

77

methods. Compared to the world-peace frontier, the toughest days west of the Pecos were baby stuff. Perhaps you can be one of the peacemakers.

Another frontier is the "getting-along-with-people frontier." We're living so close together now that we get on one another's nerves. We step on others' toes, and they step on ours. That's a much harder problem to solve than stopping the rustlers from swiping cattle from the Bar-X Ranch.

Besides these public frontiers, we all have our own personal ones. When we're young, these are the big ones: developing a healthy body; getting along with the family. Whom will I marry? What job will I pick? Will I go to college? Will I make the team?

As you get older, you have other frontiers. Even very old people have theirs. When you stop having frontiers, then you stop growing. Just as America stops growing when her people consider their nation perfect, without any need for improvement.

These frontiers are hard to see. Indeed, they're invisible. That's why you don't see them on TV and in the movies. But they're the hard ones, believe me.

You can be a frontiersman, but not in a leather-fringed jacket and shooting a Kentucky long rifle. Look around for your frontier. Then set about taming it.

42. How You Play the Game

GRANTLAND RICE WAS AMERICA'S FIRST SPORTS WRITER. HE WAS ALSO our greatest. When he died a few years ago, literally millions of people thought back over the years when they had read his thrilling accounts of World Series. Notre Dame–Army football games, the Rose Bowl Tournament, the Jack Dempsey–Gene Tunney fights of 1925 and 1926. In fact, by his great writing ability, he made these events sound more thrilling than they really were.

One small, four-line poem he wrote will probably outlast every newspaper article. It inspired me when I was a boy. I pass it on to you. In it Grantland Rice says that how we play and live is more important than the victories we win or the defeats we suffer.

It goes:

> When the One Great Scorer comes
>   To write against your name—
> He marks—not that you won or lost—
>   But how you played the game.[1]

The Great Scorer, of course, is God. The game is the game of life. And the score he puts on the scoreboard is not if you won or lost, but how much you tried and how fairly you played.

This overemphasis on results keeps millions of American boys and girls from playing sports as they should. Instead of playing for fun, doing their best, they feel inside that they *must* make the team. If they can't, they don't try. And not trying is the worst failure of all.

I realize that overwhelming competition discourages many boys and girls from trying in athletics, drama, and other extracurricular activities. For example, in a high school with 1,500 pupils, 750 of them boys, you still have a basketball team of just five players. That means the average or poor player will never get in a varsity game. What's the answer for the great majority? Not trying at all? No. It's doing your best in sports, knowing that making the team for you *is to do your best*.

Many boys and girls forget this. They say: "I don't have a chance. I won't even try." They become bleacher-sitters. They don't use their bodies, except to occupy a seat. They fail to realize that the most fun is in playing, not just playing on the team.

[1] "Alumnus Football."

How much we try—how fairly we play—is God's way of keeping score on us. To each he gives minds, bodies, brains, abilities. In the Bible Jesus told of three men who were given different amounts of money by their master. Their master took a trip. When he returned, he asked for reports on how they'd used the money. The one who had received five talents (a talent was a certain amount of money) brought in five talents more. The second man reported two more talents from his original two. The third man, who had received one talent, had done nothing with it. His master condemned him for his laziness. That story is called the parable of the talents.

It illustrates how God expects us to do our best with what he's given us. Grantland Rice put this great truth in the tiny, four-line poem just quoted:

> He marks—not that you won or lost—
> But how you played the game.

43. Are American Youth Soft?

WE IN AMERICA ARE INCLINED TO THINK THAT WE'RE THE BIGGEST, strongest, richest nation on earth. And we are in some ways. But prepare yourself for a shocker. Grab your seat.

Extensive tests of both European and American children, thousands and thousands of them, show European children far ahead of American boys and girls in muscular dexterity, which means ability to handle our bodies. Our fingers, arms, toes, legs—our whole muscular system—is not as well developed as theirs.

You may not believe this. You may say, "It's not so." But *it is* so. In fact, the president of the United States appointed a special physical fitness committee to see what could be done about it.

Why should Christians be concerned with bodily fitness and

exercise? Because our bodies are sacred. God made them. They're the house the soul lives in. If our bodies are strong and healthy, we enjoy life more. Also, we can serve God and our fellow man better. Furthermore, well people are less burden on their families and friends than are sick people.

Just why *are* American children less well developed muscularly than their European friends? Experts give these reasons: Our modern conveniences and inventions rob us of muscle use. We ride on busses and in cars instead of walking. Our grandfathers walked four miles to school and enjoyed it. Many perfectly healthy American kids won't walk ten blocks. Watch them pile off the busses after school in a typical American city. And what do they do after sitting all day in school and riding home on a bus? Why, they plop themselves down in an easy chair in front of a television set and gape at it until suppertime. Then they plop down again. Not a decent bit of exercise all day.

The Russians have now beaten us twice in the Olympics. We can give all kinds of excuses, but they beat us just the same. Could it be that we're too soft and flabby? We ought to think carefully about the reasons.

We all have exactly the same number of muscles. We can all be healthy and strong, barring a crippling disease. Naturally, not many can look like a Hercules. But we have a duty to ourselves to be healthy.

In Luke we read that Jesus "grew in wisdom and stature." He had a strong body. No single mention is made of his being sick, not one. He used his body in hard work.

I believe American children are victims of their parents' desire for luxury. But if you are a young person, don't let our national worship of ease make you a weakling. Boy or girl, you need and want a strong body. Life will be twice as good if you have one.

Take regular exercise, lots of it. Work up a sweat at least once a day. Walk instead of riding. Use that body of yours—the most marvelous machine in the world. Don't let it get rusty and creaky.

44. The Little Acorn

ONCE THERE WAS A BEAUTIFUL ACORN THAT GREW ON THE TOPMOST twig of a large oak tree. From a tiny speck of green in the spring it grew, until in the fall it became a large, beautiful brown acorn with a lustrous, shiny shell.

Being the highest acorn on the mother tree, it was the first to see the sun rise in the morning and the last to see it set at night. In fact, it saw a great deal because of its exalted position. Birds perched there, on the highest limb, to escape boys' slingshots. These birds brought endless news and chatter.

The mockingbird, with its rich repertoire of songs, gave the acorn a wonderful knowledge of music. Migratory birds, going South for the winter, brought news of arctic snows and tropic heat and places far away.

The crows, wisest of all birds, cawed away in the high branches, giving forth words of wisdom, passed on by generations of ancestors. The acorn never ceased to be amazed at their knowledge.

Indeed, this little acorn was the smartest, best-educated, and proudest acorn on the whole tree, and there were thousands of them. It looked down on its brothers and sisters, that is, when it gave them any thought at all.

One chilly fall day something terrible happened. The winds blew and rains fell. Hundreds of acorns fell to the ground. Our topmost acorn was terribly alarmed. It had presumed that life would go on forever, each day better than the previous one. Truly frightened, it asked the mother tree: "Mother, must I fall too?"

"Yes, my child," mother tree whispered gently, "all acorns must fall to the ground. When I was an acorn I fell, too, though you might not think so by looking at my strong branches now.

You might be wise to let go and fall now instead of waiting to be blown off and land poorly. But, that's up to you."

The ground was so far down. So many big limbs were in between. Besides, who wanted to abandon such a perfect position, especially when the birds were flying South, full of the latest news up North.

It clung closely to the twig. Several hard rains came. Its hold became weaker and weaker. One day mother tree said: "You had better go now, my child, and may God bless you."

The little acorn looked down. How far the ground looked! And what dangers lurked there? It grew dizzy and faint from just looking.

It closed its eyes, said a prayer, and let go. Z-z-z-z-z-z-z-z-z— the air whistled past. Then, "clickle"; it landed softly on brown leaves below.

Life below was no bed of roses. Cows trampled the ground, crushing many acorns with their hard, heavy hoofs. Pigs came and ate literally thousands, cruelly crunching their beautiful shells and eating the sweet meat inside. Squirrels picked up hundreds of others, bearing them off to some dreadful hiding place.

Our little acorn, frightened as it was, kept very still. It managed to roll under a leaf and escape detection.

Finally, snow covered the ground, and all dangers ceased. The acorn fell into a long, drowsy sleep.

Spring came. The snow melted. The sun rose higher. The acorn awoke. Poor thing, its once lovely shell was now dull and ugly. But it was alive.

Then its head began to ache terribly. What an ache!

"Help, Mother! I'm sick!" it cried.

"My child, you're not sick at all. You're perfectly well. Your headache means you're sprouting. I remember how my head hurt when I sprouted."

Now sprouting is what every acorn is meant for, if they're

lucky enough to escape the cows' hoofs, the pigs' teeth, and the squirrels' hiding places. When an acorn sprouts, its shell splits, and the seed within sends a root downward and a two-leafed twig upward. Mother tree explained all this.

"But that means *I* will die. There will be no more *me*. I don't want to change. I want to stay like I am. The world is terribly unfair!"

"Yes, my child, I felt once as you do. But look around the ground, and you'll see some of your older brothers and sisters who refused to sprout last year. Do you want to become like them?"

All around were dirty, rotten shells of what had been acorns a year before. They were so decayed that not even a pig would take notice of them. As much as our little acorn dreaded sprouting, it feared *that* kind of fate worse.

"All right, Mother," it said, "I'll sprout if I must. And if I should become half as lovely and strong as you, I won't even mind the pain."

That night it rained, and the next day the acorn's shell split open. How it did hurt! Then, there came a wonderful and happy feeling to the little acorn.

Weeks and months passed. Fall came and found a strong little oak tree three inches high, strongly rooted in the ground.

Today, if you'll visit the spot, you will find two trees. One, the mother tree, is getting old. Before many years it will fall to the ground or be cut down by woodcutters.

Beside it is a straight, slender young oak. Birds perch in its high limbs. Some build their nests there. Others bring interesting news as they migrate North and South.

Because it dared fall to the ground, because it chose to give up its coat and cease being an acorn, because it was willing to grow, even though it hurt, our little acorn is now this lovely tree.

45. Let God Shine Through Your Life

IN THE PEABODY MUSEUM AT YALE UNIVERSITY IN NEW HAVEN, Connecticut, is a wonderful collection of mineral rocks.

They are in a small, darkened room. Actually, at first glance, they are very ordinary looking rocks. Should you see them lying by the roadside or path, many are so ordinary looking that you'd never have given them a second glance. A visitor to the museum might well ask: "What are these rocks doing here? Why, I've seen nicer looking ones than that at home!"

And, actually, a great many *are* exactly the same kind you can pick up in almost any section of the United States without paying a penny for the privilege. Brown, yellow, black, grey, white—most of the mineral rocks in Peabody Museum are ordinary looking.

But, press the button by the display case, and what a change! Instantly these dull-looking pieces of rock are transformed. They glow with unbelievably lovely colors—rose, pink, soft purple, green, lavender, blue, grey-blue, and dozens of other colors. These colors, more beautiful than the mind of man can conceive, all seem to come from inside the minerals.

And what makes the change? Well, a very common kind of light bulb in the top of the display case. Not the kind we use in our homes, not that common, but an ultraviolet light bulb, the kind which gives off a light ray too blue or too purple for the human eye to see. The ultraviolet light has a mysterious effect on the mineral rocks. What the process is, I don't know.

Considerable scientific knowledge of light physics would be required to explain the change. But anybody can see the change and vouch for the fact that the change in the appearance of these rocks does occur.

You might say we are like these rocks in many ways. So many of us are just average. To other people we may even appear dull, unattractive, and not worth taking a second look at. That's the truth, even though we appear pretty nice to ourselves.

But a mysterious, quick, and lovely change can take place in our own lives. How?

By our letting God's light, his love, his great spirit, shine through us. Like the rocks, which need an outside source to make them glow so brilliantly, human beings are most attractive when they allow God to influence them.

We are different from the rocks in that we can refuse God if we wish. Rock minerals in a glass case have no power to prevent the ultraviolet light being turned on them.

But you and I *can* say to ourselves, to others, and to God: "I'm choosing to be mean, selfish, stingy, self-centered, and indifferent to God and man!" And a lot of people do just that. Not in so many words, but by neglect and failing to choose the best in life.

As we get older and the natural attractiveness of youth fades, we need the unfailing radiance that comes from inside. What we are inside makes the difference then. And what we are inside depends mainly on how we let God affect us. Do we refuse him, or do we ask him every day to guide, lead, instruct, and inspire us?

You can be dull and unattractive. Or you can be more and more attractive each year you live. God can make the difference, *if you let him.*

46. *Paying Off Your Debts*

WE'RE ALL HEAVILY IN DEBT. I AM. YOU ARE. WE ALL ARE. BUT HOW, you might ask.

Here's how: Practically every advantage, every blessing, every

cherished possession or ideal we have came to us through somebody else's hard work.

But, you can object, don't I work hard for what I get? I don't
owe anything to anybody! You're absolutely wrong.

Here are just a few items for which you're in debt: our American form of government, embodying dozens of political ideas it
took thousands of years to develop and millions of lives laid down
for their achievements. The church, with all it offers. Religious
freedom. The Bible, which it took centuries to write. Thousands
of men died so that we might have the freedom to read it.

Your warm home. You don't live in a cave, shivering over a
fire, suffering from cold all winter. Our cave-man ancestors did.
Now we have warm houses heated by automatic furnaces.

And what about your health? Two hundred years ago you'd
have had only one chance in two of living one year after birth.
Chances are you'd have only fallen to smallpox, pneumonia, or
some other dread disease before you were twenty, had you sur-
vived your first year.

And just recently—the Salk vaccine, so long awaited. And now
many parents are too lazy to take their children to get this anti-
polio preventative. Why, just a bare five years ago parents became desperate when polio struck their community! Now we
take for granted this great discovery by Dr. Jonas Salk.

Other disease preventatives that took years and years of research didn't just happen. Somebody sweated night and day. Because of their dedication, we enjoy health.

I could go on all day listing our debts. Our Pure Food and
Drug Act, our great system of highways, our freedom to move
from one state to another without tariffs or passport, our freedom
to attend whatever church we want, our right to vote for the
candidate we think best. All these blessings we owe to somebody
else.

How can we pay these debts? Well, actually we can't pay the
people to whom we owe them. But we can do something better.

We can so work and live that *our descendants will owe us debts*. How?

We can leave our church, our schools, our cities, towns, and nation better than we found them. We can add to our great inheritance. So that people coming later will say: "They left us a fine world."

Otherwise we will be parasites. A parasite is a plant or animal that lives off other plants or animals. For example, mistletoe lives off trees. Its seed lodges high in a tree crotch, sinks its roots in, and draws from the tree's sap. It depends entirely on the tree for life. It receives all and gives back nothing.

Yes, we are all heavily in debt to others and to God. We can't possibly pay them off. But we can leave the world richer for our being here.

47. Don't Be Afraid to Daydream

EVER GET "LOST IN THE CLOUDS" WITHOUT STEPPING INTO AN AIRplane? Or have you ever been "a thousand miles away" without moving your feet? Some call this being absent minded—thinking about a subject the outside observer could never guess.

Or has your teacher or a parent ever said, "A penny for your thoughts," and then you suddenly "came to" and jerked yourself out of a dreamworld of your own into the world just around you?

We've all had these experiences. Naturally, excessive daydreaming can lead to complete inaction. A boy can dream about being a star quarterback or a high-scoring basketball forward and allow his dreams to take the place of hard practice. Such a fellow winds up in the bleachers. Dreaming alone is not enough.

Or a girl can daydream that she's the most popular girl in school, with boys flocking around her, begging for dates. But such dreaming doesn't replace friendliness, good cheer, health, pep, ability to look one's best, interest in others—the qualities that make an attractive personality. A selfish girl may daydream until doomsday and still have no friends. Effort must be expended in friendship.

Still, without daydreams we have no ideals, no goals, no heights to climb. Charles Lindbergh dreamed of flying the Atlantic Ocean alone. The idea fascinated him. He determined to be the first to do so. But the dream was only the beginning.

If you read his books, you know how carefully he supported this dream with months of grueling preparation. Raising the money for a plane, charting a course, getting financial backers, waiting for just the right weather, knowing exactly how to get a plane heavily loaded with gasoline, off the ground. Finally, that take-off from New York and the landing in Paris some thrity-three hours later—the greatest airplane flight in history.

Another ocean-crossing over four centuries earlier—in reverse direction—from Europe to America took a dream followed by hard work. Christopher Columbus had almost the same experiences as Charles Lindbergh. First, a great idea. Then, begging for money. Then, making preparations. And all the while that great dream in the background, driving him on. We know the rest.

Woodrow Wilson dreamed of a great, world-wide federation of nations that would keep peace. He died before he saw any such organization, but not before he had literally given his life to promote the idea. Today we have the United Nations, not all that Wilson had dreamed of, but a big step toward it. Had he not dreamed and then worked, it is not likely the U.N. would exist today.

Dream your dreams while you're young. Don't be afraid to dream big ones. Make them tower over you. Make them worthy of giving your life to.

Jesus must have dreamed, as a boy, of a world without hate— a world filled with peace and love. He gave his life toward such a dream. We don't have a perfect world yet, but take away the life and death of Jesus Christ, and what a dismal world it would be.

Dream your dreams. And, then, back them up with hard work.

Dreams have a way of coming true—if you make them.

48. How Much Does God Love Us?

ANY ANSWER TO THIS QUESTION WOULD BE WRONG. WHY?

Because we can't measure anything God does.

Take distance for instance. How far is it to the farthest star or galaxy of stars God made billions of years ago? We don't know, nor will we ever know. Our most powerful telescope, the two-hundred-inch one at Mount Palomar, California, isn't strong enough to focus on the most distant galaxy. And remember that each galaxy contains millions and millions of stars the size of our sun.

How many grains of sand on the earth's beaches and in her sandpits? Nobody will know ever. But God knows.

How many waves this very second on all the oceans, lakes, rivers, and ponds? What a crazy question! But God knows how many.

How many hairs on your head? Anybody who would waste time counting them ought to have *his* head examined, but for another reason. But God knows how many. Jesus told us he did.

How many feathers on each sparrow in the world? How many stars in the sky? How many snowflakes and raindrops are falling on the earth this very second? How many people are there being born, dying, or getting over sickness this moment? You would think we could answer such a simple question as: "How many people are living?" but we can't. We can't even say, and be sure, but how many people are alive in the United States, or even in your own state.

But God can answer each of these questions!

Why? Because he's God. He is without limit in his knowledge, his power, and his love.

Not even our own parents know all about us. Think of the things you think and do that they know absolutely nothing about. But God knows. Why? Because he's God.

How much does he love us? More than all the great minds of the world can imagine. More than our parents love us, or our sweethearts, or our best friend.

Compare what we know with what God knows, and you know then how much he loves us. More than we can possibly imagine.

He cared so much for us that he sent Jesus Christ, his Son, to suffer pain and hardship and finally be crucified just to show us, as much as our puny minds can understand, how great is his love.

Do you know anybody you would die for? The list is short, isn't it? But Jesus died for us all. He excluded nobody. Not even the worst criminal. He would die for the meanest murderer who ever lived. He even died for Judas Iscariot, the traitor.

If you ever feel that nobody loves you, then you're absolutely wrong. For God loves you. His love never fails. It is as strong when you're bad as when you're good. Jesus told us this too.

What wonderful news this was! Men felt lonely, lost, and without hope. Only the privileged few felt God would take care of them in this world and the next. Then Jesus, God's own Son, came with the great news that our heavenly Father loves us—each and all. Even you and me.

How much does God love us? The biggest dictionary hasn't enough words to provide the right answer. We only know this—that he does and always will love us, his own children. God's love will never fail. Always remember that.

49. For Girls Only
—How to Be Beautiful

EVERY GIRL WANTS TO BE A BEAUTIFUL WOMAN. AND, BELIEVE IT OR not, every girl can be! How?

First, it's no trick. It can't be done overnight. Or in a beauty parlor. Nor can this beauty we talk about be applied with a powder puff or even come from the most expensive lipstick or rouge. Nor will the most fragrant Paris perfume costing $100 an ounce bring the kind of beauty which increases every passing year.

Most girls are naturally attractive. With all our good medical care, well-balanced diets, and widespread knowledge of the rules of health, our American girls have many advantages over their mothers and grandmothers. So many, many of them are truly lovely.

But the beauty that comes from youth is a fragile thing. It can fade like the color of the rose or the dew on the morning-glory. And when the original loveliness of girlhood goes, it is gone forever—unless! *Unless* it is replaced with a loveliness that comes from the inside.

What makes a lovely woman? Naturally, paint, powder, and lipstick do help. Attractive clothing and visits to the beauty parlor do their part too.

But, all around us, we see the most horrible, gloomy, unattractive faces with all these artificial aids doing their best, but not doing enough to hide an inner ugliness of mind and soul. As the years pass, we show more and more what we truly are inside. And since every woman wants to be beautiful, she had best be the right kind of person inside. All the drugstore creams and powders in the world can't cover up hate or worry or selfishness.

Some of the most beautiful adult women I know were not considered such good-lookers as girls. Frequently they weren't the ones who had the most dates or phone calls. But they did have a sweetness of spirit inside, which showed more and more on their faces.

On the other hand, I know some women who were truly beautiful twenty years ago. But selfishness, too much spoiling, greed—yes, and sometimes indulgence—have taken away that beauty. It has been replaced by worry lines, wrinkles, anxious looks, and a fear of growing old. Now that they've lost the beauty of youth, they've nothing inside to replace it. Their chief asset is gone forever. They're bankrupt.

To you who are younger—what women are the most beautiful to you? I suspect your answer is based on your observation of what women are the finest Christians. You have no idea what they resembled twenty, thirty, and forty years ago. So, your answer must come from what you observe right now.

True beauty can survive even terrible physical suffering. I know one woman whose waking hours are spent in a wheel chair and who sleeps in a specially constructed bed. Even crippling polio can't blot out a radiant face which literally glows with patience, love, and cheer.

Yes, you can be a beautiful woman. But your beauty must come from inside you, not from the drugstore. Think great and good thoughts. Love God and your fellow man. Give your time and talent to serve others.

And this we can depend on—you will be a beautiful woman!

50. Why Protestants Believe in Religious Liberty

IMAGINE THIS HAPPENING IN AMERICA, IF YOU CAN: A FAMILY decides they want to change churches. Only one church exists in the town where they live. So, they say: "Since we no longer believe in this church, we will worship God at home and invite our friends who believe the same way to join us." The first time they hold a service at their home, police break through the front door, drag them to jail without trial, and hold them until they're sentenced to prison.

What a wild, impossible idea! you might say.

Only it wasn't wild and impossible several hundred years ago. That's the way it *was* done. Individuals who didn't attend the church of the majority or of the king of the area *were* taken to jail. As a matter of fact, literally thousands of persons were murdered because they didn't conform to rigid religious laws or say they would attend church against their beliefs.

Martin Luther, Zwingli, Huss, Tyndale, Cranmer—these are just a few of the leaders of the great Protestant Reformation. Five hundred years ago practically all Christians belonged to the Roman Catholic Church. Then men like the ones we just named began to think: Religion and salvation come from God, not from a church. Let's study the Bible and see what it says, instead of taking the word of church officials. For saying and writing such ideas these men were persecuted. Some were killed. One of my own relatives, John Hooper, an Englishman, was burned at the stake by "Bloody Mary," queen of England, for being a Protestant.

Because so many Protestants were killed, imprisoned, hounded from home, driven from their country, and branded as heathen, they began to have this idea: Why not create a land where all men can worship God according to their own consciences?

Not all Protestants believed this. Some of them, even in America, the New World, wanted to force others to believe *their* way. But they soon saw their mistake. They joined with such great men as William Penn and Roger Williams in establishing true religious freedom for men of all churches or of no church.

They had been treated so shamefully that they wanted nobody else to endure the hardships they suffered. No longer should innocent, God-fearing families lie shivering with fright at night, afraid that police would arrest them for reading the Bible, or singing hymns, or talking together about Jesus Christ. Neither they nor Roman Catholics nor Jews nor anybody of any creed or religion should be punished for following their beliefs. Also, they said, it was wrong for the government to take tax money from citizens by force and give it to any church, however good that church might be.

So, they created a new nation, the United States of America, where no church group persecutes another, where all men may worship God in their own way, where tax money is not turned over to churches, where we can sleep soundly at night without fear of arrest for our religious convictions.

Protestants are not the only ones who now believe in religious freedom. Gradually other churches are turning to our position as the right one. They know that love of God cannot be forced on men. We must love and worship him because we want to.

Be proud of your Protestant heritage. Because of it Americans worship God in many ways without conflict. May the day come when people everywhere can do the same.